Rarities & Wonders: Plays

Praise for *Frontieres Sans Frontieres*

10 BEST THEATRICAL PRODUCTIONS OF THE YEAR! In a year and a country so committed to deadly earnestness, Phillip Howze's delightfully dark satire of our penchant for tragedy porn — and our self-important desire to feel like morally superior global citizens — felt like a bracing gust of wind... Linguistically acrobatic and piercingly funny, *Frontieres* is a whip-smart modern burlesque that deserves a wider audience.
— Sarah Holdren, *New York Magazine*

★★★★ CRITIC'S PICK! Before you read any description — heck, before you read this review — let me assure you that Phillip Howze's *Frontieres Sans Frontieres* is a comedy. You might get the wrong idea when you see that it's about refugee kids playing in rubble, learning to beg, gaming the World Health Organization and succumbing to any number of predators. You might expect a downer. But Howze's exciting piece is actually a savage burlesque, a clear-eyed bouffon treatment of war... Howze has already achieved something titanic by telling us that today, Mother Courage is a child. Even Brecht didn't have the steel for that.
— Helen Shaw, *Time Out New York*

A vibrant new play... a kaleidoscope of funny, absurd displays of humanity swinging, pendulum-like, between the mundane and the magical, the minuscule and the grand.
— Carly Fineman, *Bushwick Daily*

In Phillip Howze's hilarious, heart-wrenching, and sometimes scabrous *Frontieres Sans Frontieres*... three stateless kids take center stage. They speak a creatively styled English that tickles the listener's ear and could only be uttered by those for whom English is a second language. The plucky trio live, dance, and make mischief in a garbage heap, where they encounter a number of well-intentioned adult buffoons who try to improve the lot of the youngsters... Howze's off-kilter language, delivered in accents that bounce among Swedish and Russian and many cadences in between, creates an infectious energy... Despite, or perhaps because of, its comedic tone, *Frontieres Sans Frontieres* also manages to deeply unsettle. The adult characters who pass through the garbage heap create an arch parade of poverty tourism, and they have the satirical sting of the uncomfortable truth.

— Eliza Bent, *TDF Stages*

Playwright Phillip Howze is a name you want to know if you like your theater to have some social electricity. Personally, I prefer a little sizzle with a 90-120 minute commitment to a live performance (I can take naps at home for free thank you very much)... *Frontieres* tackles issues of social justice and human rights on an international scale through the lens of three stateless youth in a country both foreign and familiar... it's timely. *Frontieres* seems to be mirroring our right now.

— Daaimah Mubashshir, *Culturebot*

A brightly colored comic fantasia on cultural imperialism... Mr. Howze's intelligent, unruly and intermittently wonderful play is grounded in experience... There is much beauty in this abundance.

— Laura Collins-Hughes, *The New York Times*

Praise for *all of what you love and none of what you hate*

★★★★! The powerful impact of *all of what you love and none of what you hate* is immense, shattering, shocking, and paradigm shifting... Edris Cooper-Anifowoshe has taken Phillip Howze's brilliantly conceived script and directed at a pace and a level of intensity that at times takes one's breath away... all play starring roles in a production team that has joined this cast and the director in producing a bone-chilling evening.
    — Eddie Reynolds, *Theatre Eddys*

This is the most provocative play I have seen this year... It's also called a symphony in 23 movements written for light, sound, projections and people. The production features three outstanding actors, and all are superb in their roles... It's a world of miscommunication in social media, self-help, and bad advice... Phillip Howze's drama is full of emotions — anger, hopelessness, acquiescence, obliviousness, infidelity, and annoyance... [it's] sharp and incisive.
    — Richard Connema, *Talkin' Broadway*

It's a psychological adventure, rare on the stage and tricky to execute... We feel as though we've been plunged into the dream world, where real conflicts find horrid and unrealistic solutions... This is a lovely tone poem of a play, mapping the unconscious... a rare fusion of internal and external pressures — demonstrating abandonment and unfeeling in a contemporary electronic wasteland... Watch for more innovations from Phillip Howze, who is attempting to project dangerous inner turmoil in a turbulent, divided, and far from equal United States.
    — Barry David Horwitz, *Theatrius*

Copyright © 2022 Phillip Howze

All rights reserved. Except for brief passages quoted in newspaper, magazines, radio, or television reviews, no part of this book may be reproduced in an form or by any means, electronic or mechanical, including photocopying or recording, or by an information storage and retrieval system, without permission in writing from the publisher.

Professionals and amateurs are hereby warned that this material, being fully protected under the Copyright Laws of the United States of America, and all other countries of the Berne and Universal Copyright Conventions, is subject to a performance royalty. All rights, including professional and amateur stage productions, recitation, lecturing, public reading, motion picture, radio broadcasting, television and the rights of translation into foreign languages are expressly reserved. Particular emphasis is placed on the question of public readings and all uses of this book by educational institutions, permissions for which must be secured from the author's representative:
Emma Feiwel, William Morris Endeavor Entertainment, 11 Madison Avenue, 18th Floor, New York, NY 10010, (212) 903-1100.

RARITIES & WONDERS: PLAYS
Phillip Howze

CONTENTS

Inquiry 10
Conjecture 16
462 Halsey 22
Self Portrait #2 44
Self Portrait #5 60
Self Portrait #7 68
Self Portrait #28 82
all of what you love and none of what you hate 90
Production Credits 169

Inquiry

Someone said to me recently: what is a play? And I said to myself, what *is* a play?

Is it a person, a place, a thing? Is it the concept or the text or the production? Is a play defined by the one who makes it or by the one who sees it? Who is the seer, then? What is a play in the world, to a world of people who don't know what a play is? Is it written, spoken, read, performed, scored, ideated — is it authored? Are we, too, authored, the authors — us — by the world?

How does a play exist in the world in which we live today and is that, or are plays, changing? Are the ways of the world being questioned? Who are the players? Do we trust the authors? What is real and what isn't?

Who is our authority?

Ask my mother am I more like my mother or like the world, or like myself? Who am I — who is making me — who has made me make what I'm making, me? My surroundings? Do I owe someone somewhere something?

These words, are they worthy? Are these words — is this a work of art? I often wonder: what is the *work* of art? To ask? To affirm? To resist? To remake? To turn what's outside inward — to inquire? Is the work working out our insides? Is it churning our guts, or simply sating us? Are we being gifted a balanced diet?

Is art a gift we give? Can a gift be a rattlesnake wrapped in a bow?

She said, but what does that mean? How can what we do be made meaningful to someone who doesn't know what it is we do? — how are we making meaning? I ask, does meaning really matter? Where did you get this desire for justification, from your mother? From the adolescent lust for a "done good," or an A+ average?

Is your art an equation to be averaged? Is achievement a process or a result?

Did your mother take you to the theater to see self-affirming plays? Yet what if she didn't? Did you witness your image reflected in a scientific anthropology onstage and is that why you became inspired to write, to further justify your existence? But what if you weren't? What if you were of the tribe born from the wild, extemporaneous, wretched world? Why have those children been orphaned?

Can destruction have dignity?

My particular plays only feature people of color (simply imagine the premise of a play-world populated only by people of color?) whose characters are often revealed to the spectator in tempestuous, theatrical and disruptive modes — what does that tell you about me?

Whose idealism are we discussing?

In any given theater on any given evening, do the well-mannered outnumber the ill-mannered? Do more people "get it" than don't? Does that make it more likely or less likely that we will have authentic dialogue, discussion and debate — since we're all pretty much on the same page with how we feel about it? Why is everything so terribly inevitable?

Is making a play equivalent to making your mother and the authorities proud of you? Is this why in the theater, at large, a so-called realism — which is to say art which reaffirms a digestible history and a relatable politics — is more easily embraced than work which asks troubling or meandering or unanswerable questions?

Is a play a palliative? Is the theater about feeling safe — is this what realism reminds us of, the womb?

Does the world seem safe to you right now? What do you imagine I, a young Black person, feel about my level of safety in America? How do you think I feel about power and dominance? Is realism a distinction that allows Blackness to fit safely inside of an explicable black box? Is the American theater prepared to express how the plethora of young writers of color see the world today? Or will these writers be forced to retrofit their work into safety mechanisms for the would-be sated?

Which leads me to wonder: is realism an analog for white America? Is that why realism is so dominant in the American theater?

Historically speaking, people who looked like me were forced to serve and service most of our time-honored American institutions (the academy, industry, the domestic household) not the other way around, right?

Exactly, he said, and isn't therein the argument to be made
in favor of realism? Couldn't it be considered a form
of self-preservation, relevant precisely because it provides
a kind of reparation to groups of people who for centuries
have had to remix, borrow, adapt and remake culture
in order to outrun their bodies and bodies of work being
stolen? What in the world is a play to a world of folks
who have been disenfranchised, disembodied — whose
histories have been forcefully appropriated or stereotyped
or parodied for so long? How are we forged under
the threat of extinction?

Aren't you interested in this conversation?

Why do actors sometimes say, "I was inside of it, man,
I had no idea what I was doing until weeks after the show
closed?" Isn't that curious?

Is a play a question or an answer? Isn't a question a kind
of collective bargaining agreement between all interested
parties, an attempt to create a social responsibility, a
joint obligation to consider the variables instead of always
attempting to solve for x? Is the theater capable of
celebrating a not knowing? Who will shelter the wretched?

Have we created space to allow everyone to get "inside
of it, man?" Will we welcome art that questions what *is*
even is?

Are we interested in asking, or are we too busy searching
for answers?

Conjecture

It needs to be
more accessible

                        I'm sorry?

More people

                      ———

— need access
Generally
In general.
The general population.
How are you helping
them, you know?

                      Is that what I should
                      be doing?

Not specifically, but
generally.
A helping hand
it's always better than a
biting one.

                      But.
                      Hands don't bite.

No.
I think I was thinking
about that saying.
On biting the hand.

            ———

You know?
The one

            ———

Don't bite the hand that
that
that

                                                What does that
                                                have to do with

It doesn't — This isn't
— I'm not really talking
about us, about people
like us, you and me. I'm.
More other people.
You have to make it clear.
And intentional.
Helpful.

                                                You think it's — I'm
                                              unhelpful

Yes and no.

                                                ———

It is and it isn't.

>	So
>	is it, or isn't it?

It's just not very specific
not specific enough in the
ways people are used to
you know it's not broadly
specific.

———

There should be a thing
about it it's about, that
that's more specific
in general. Generally
that reminds people
of something
specific-like. Like:
Martin Luther King, Jr.

———

Okay that's not what
I mean specifically.
But you know what
I mean.

>	That. It should be more
>	like Martin Luther King
>	Jr.

No God no.
NO.
Like: You.
You. Do. You.

———

And like, maybe
wedge in
like
that thing
that other people do.
You know?

                                                  No.

See it's just I can see
I see myself
in need of doing a lot of
explaining
on your behalf.
For you.

———

———

                                            Or not. You could not
                                            do that, and just
                                            let people ponder.

Yeah. But, no.

                    No but yeah
                    they're smart.
                    They'll figure
                    something out.

———

                            ———

No.

                    No?

Yeah.
No.
                    O.

———
                            ———

———

                    Are you sure about that?

462 Halsey

Players: A
          B

I

There is no chair.
The chair is not there.
Two people, A and B, stare in different directions.

A   I think this is where the chair was.
    (*Unsure.*)
    I think this is where the chair was.
    (*Unsure.*)
    I think this is where the chair was.

B   It was here.

A   —.
    No it wasn't. Was it?

B   It was.

A   It was?
    —.
    It wasn't.

B   It was

A   It isn't.

B   That doesn't mean it wasn't.

A   That doesn't mean it was.
    —.
    I think the chair was here I think the chair was

        here is where I think the chair was.
        I think the chair was here and the lamp was there.
        I think the chair was here, and the lamplight here,
        and the curio there.

B   The chair. Was here.
        The lamp, the light that you think was here, was
        there.

A   Nono nononono

B   Aaanndd the curio was where you thought the
        chair was.

A   (?)
        Well —
        —.
        Well.
        THIS is where the fireplace stood.
        And here, where the firewood laid.
        And there that was where the the the. The firebrand
        it —

B   What firebrand?

A   The fire (*Pokes.*)
        The fire (*Pokes.*) brand.

B   That's not what you mean I don't think.

A   You know what I mean the uh, the stick
        — theeee —

the stick with the (*Hook.*) that (*Claws.*) — to
the — fire.

B   The stick that stokes the fire?

A   Yes the stick that stokes the fire — theeee fire stick
stoker. This is where it was. Remember?

B   —.
Fire iron
It was called a fire iron — is. It is called. That.

A   Well clearly you know what I meant

B   How do you know what I know

A   I don't I just I know.
—.
What would she have called it?

B   What would she have called it?
—.
Poker?

A   Yeah.
Fire place poker. Or. Fire stick stoker.
—.
But I like fire iron too. It has a kind of (*"w w w"*).
FiirreeIirrooon. It makes a shape, in your mouth.
Feels, I don't know, funny-sounding.
—.
The chair that was here was old-world. Weathered.

It had hand-me-down scratches.
One leg was brushed-knickel, or silver?
That one leg was a replacement leg.
I loved staring at that little leg.
Something about it. Right there beside the original wood.
Something about it.
—.
FiirreeIirrooon.

B   —.
You are so strange.

A   No I'm not

B   You are. You used to be

A   No I wasn't

B   You were

A   Why would you say that

B   Because you were I remember you are

A   No you don't
No I'm not.

B   The chair was here, the FiirreeIirrooon was here.
I have a photographic memory.
I remember things.

A   What's my phone number?

B   —.
    —.

A   See! See!
    You don't remember everything

B   Nobody remembers phone numbers anymore.

A   You'd be lost without me

B   Unless we were both lost.
    With each other.
    Unless that's where we are.
    —.
    The chair was never there.

A   Ok fine.

B   Ok.

A   Ok then. Photographic Memory.

B   Ok

A   Then.
    Then what was here then?

B   What was where?

A   There? What was there.

B   Here?

A   Yes.

B   When?

A   Then.

B   Hmm.
—.

A   —.

B   Ok.
—.
Mmha! The ottoman.

A   Nope.

B   Really? The magazine basket?

A   (*Laughs, shakes head.*)

B   Here?

A   Yeah.

B   Well. If here was the firebrand...

A   Ha. Ha. Funny.

B   The magazine basket, then? The fish tank?
        The umbrella holder.
        —. The magazine basket.

A   The dining room table.

B   The dining room table?

A   Yes. This was his recliner. This was her loveseat.

B   Then that's where the kitchen was?

A reorients B.

A   That's where the kitchen was.

B   I thought you said the table was there?

A   It was.

B   Then that way is east.

A   Which way does the sun set fool? West.
        That's the way you're pointing.

B   Oh.

A   The dining room was sunlit in the morning, the
        kitchen in the late afternoon. That's why she
        would put her window herbs on the table and not on
        the window.

B   The dining room table. With its prickly centerpiece of chives and tarragon and spearmint.

A   Weeds. Remember that's what he said he used to call them weeds?
"Why these weeds on the table?"
"Why these weeds in the middle of the table, I'm trying to eat here."
"It's like I'm eating near the unmowed grass next to these weeds."

B   The grass: Remember how he used to make you mow the grass? Even it was a hundred degrees outside he would make you mow. You would complain, complain.

A   He never had you mow the grass, I remember that.

B   That's not true

A   It is.

B   No it isn't. I mowed the grass. Like... once.
—.
Naw. No naw I never mowed the grass.

A   See.

B   Ok ok.

A   See see — this is where I'd be. Sweating, swearing under my breath. A hundred degrees PUSHING that push-mower. Pretty sure if I didn't die from fatigue then, for sure, from heatstroke. Trying to will myself to faint for real that way he'll find me out there, limp and lifeless, and have to rush my feeble little body to Woodhull Hospital feeling guilty all the way. Begging my forgiveness, "Please don't die!" "I admit I've made mistakes." "I shouldnta had you out here suffering while I watched reruns on TV." "Please forgive me you must!" And then, while crying tears of regret over my drooping, half-dead limbs, he'd lean down, whispering into my ear a promise to never make me mow the grass ever again. And alas, I would miraculously recover.

Beat.

B   It's gotten a little.
Overrun out here.

A   That it has.

A bug buzzes near B's head.

B   And all the —.
This is where her garden was too?

A   That it was.

B   So this is where the greens were?
That's right — These were the sweet potatoes.
There were the onions, the garlic, the radish.

A   There was where you tried to grow a watermelon.

B   A lotta luck I had with that.

A   You weren't born with a green thumb, I remember.

B   More like a poison thumb.

A   Speaking of, who am I?

B puts thumb in mouth.

B   O stop.

A   Who am I, at three.
Who am I at five, at eight even.

B   Come on stop.

A   You sucked your thumb until you were eleven years old.

B   You couldn't ride a bike until you were twelve.

A   You didn't like to take baths. Ever

B   You thought the toilet was a monster that ate your poop.

A You believed in Santa Claus

B You believed in Santa Claus too.

A I still believe in Santa Claus
I still believe in the tooth fairy.
This is where my bed was.
This is where I put my little teeth under the pillow.
This is where the tooth fairy took my teeth and let me two nickels.
—

Across the street was the five and ten where I took my two nickels to buy four hard candies.
Next door to that was the hatmakers.

B Here is the firewood.
Here is the fireplace.
Here is the fire iron poker stoker.
Here is the mantel over the fireplace.

A Down the block was the wall where we used to play handball and across from that, the fire hydrant we cracked open in the summertime. Almost everyday we were chased down that street by Mrs. Jenkins' bloodhound. Mrs. Jenkins' bloodhound was nicknamed Dr. Ugly because he was both very smart and very, very ugly.

B   Here are the photos of family and friends and neighbors. Of holidays, and anniversaries, and high school graduations. Here is the door that leads to the hallway that leads to the bedrooms that rests the elders.

A   What elders?

B   The elders.

A   Where are the elders?

B   There.

A   Where

B   There.

A   Where?

II

A and B are elders.
The chair is there.

B —.
   Where did my chair go?

A What?

B My chair?

A What chair?

B The chair that was there,
   Where'd it go.

A —.
   I don't know what you're —

B The chair.

A —.
   You're gonna have to clarify wha —

B The chair.

A —.

B There.
   Was.
   A chair. There.

A   Are you feeling. All right?

B   I'm fine.

A   May I feel your? (*Hand to forehead.*)
         Or. (*Checks pulse.*)
         Maybe (*Ear to heart.*)

B   I'm fine.

A   Are you?
         Are you.

B   ——.
         I think I am.
         (*Near the chair.*)
         I would like to sit down somewhere.
         I should sit down.
         I'll do that.

A   Where? There is nowhere. Not for you.
         There is nowhere to sit right now

B   HA!, so. There was a chair there —— HA!

A   Well

B   You said it, There's nowhere to sit.

A   Well

B   You said it, There's nowhere for you.

A   What I said was where?
Where if you were to sit. Where?
You want to sit on the floor?

B   (*To a spectator in a chair.*)
I could sit there

A   There?

B   Yeah. Right there.

A   No you couldn't.

B   Why not?

A   Because there's someone sitting there.

B   There's someone sitting there?

A   Yeah.

B   Who?

A   I don't know. Somebody.

B   I don't —.
There isn't anybody sitting there.

A   There is someone sitting, right there.

B   —.
No there is isn't.

A   Fine. Sit there then and see.

B   But where is the chair?
I don't see the chair.

A   You're as blind as a bat.

B   You're as blind as a bat!

A   You are always seeing things that are not there.
You are always NOT seeing things that ARE there.
This is the very definition of: blind as a bat.

B   You are always forgetting where I put things.
You should remember where I put things that way at least one of us knows.

A   I know things. I remember things.
You worry too much.
—.
I remember where I put my keys this morning.
I remember who won the World Series.
I remember the name of our current President.
I remember to look both ways before crossing the street.
I remember how much it cost to ride the subway.

B   The price just went up

A   It did? Again?!

B   Yep.
—.
Was my chair even ever right there?
Am I remembering wrongly?

A   Do you want the truth?

B   What I want is to remember things the way they were.

A   Well. Well then. It probably was there at some point I'm sure.

B   So where is it now?!

A   Calm down.

B   Don't tell me to calm down.

A   Then, settle down.

B   Don't tell me to settle down.

A   Then. Carry on then.

B   Why can't I remember anything?
What's wrong with my memory?

A   —.
Stop worrying. I'll try to remember things for the both of us. Okay?

B I just want to have a seat.
  —.
  You won't remember the things I want you to know.

A You worry too much. Sometimes. Sometimes, you just gotta make the best of standing.
  You know?
  I know. Now stop worrying.
  I know a place. Ain't nobody worrying.
  Ain't nobody crying. Ain't no smiling faces.
  Schom on, schom on. I'll take you there.
  —.
  Wanna dance?

The Staples Sisters: "I'll Take You There" plays.
They dance.
They disappear.

III

The empty chair, the one that is there.
It speaks.

THE CHAIR Hello?
Hello?
(*Sighs.*) The life of a chair. Hello? Where are they? Where did they all go? The life of a chair is often like this. Longing. Lonely. Better I suppose than some but still. Lonely nonetheless. Better I warrant than being chopped up for firewood. Better I imagine than being set outside to rot. Someone once told me that that's what happens. When you have no more usefulness you get tossed away. But I don't know. Who wouldn't have use for me? I'm wise. I got jokes, I'm good-looking. And I'm for real even, not some imitation. I often wonder what happens to the ones who disappear. Do you know? Can you recall? Have you forgotten?

END OF PLAY.

Self Portrait #2

Players: a SPEAKER, Black
           and, a speaker, black
           and, a HYPE MAN

Note: The SPEAKER speaks into a corded
           microphone which is not amplified.

           The HYPE MAN, unseen, deejays
           the corresponding sounds to/through
           the speaker:
           KICK BOOM KICK BOOM SNAPPER
           SNAPPER KICK BOOM SNAPPER

SELF PORTRAIT #2

*A SPEAKER enters with a corded microphone
(and, perhaps, a mic stand).*

The microphone is never on but it seems to trail to a hidden speaker/PA system.

Unseen, a HYPE MAN will soon deejay sounds via the speaker/PA system.

The SPEAKER waits for plaudits.

The SPEAKER waits.

Unbeknownst to them, they have a little white toilet tissue stuck to the bottom of their shoe.

The SPEAKER smiles.

Ahem.

The SPEAKER caresses the mic stand a bit.

The caress is an uneasy or a pathological or a ritual stroking, up and down.

Ahem.

Smiles.

When the SPEAKER speaks, it is utterly deadpan throughout.

SPEAKER   I'm not an actor. So uhm. Um ahhhh. I'm
going through a thing. I don't know
what it is, exactly. But. About, a year ago I
was sitting you know not not on a but uh,
in place in a place, which is approximately
really an approximation sort of of where
I was last year, in the middle middling. And
I was in there alone I mean not in inside
of there but in that place and meanwhile he
thinks to myself: how am I going to
get outta here? Get through this. By myself
— am I gonna make it? I got the strength
to, to, The guts to push through?? And it'd
be bad luck in fact it would it would —
suckluck — to stay there, be found. In an
inbetween place, there — there, I don't
know maybe maybe it's actually not really
as bad as, as, horrible as — in a Srebrenica
kind of way, or — um um an act of,
or — it could be worse. Domestic terror?
While on the toilet?? Yikes. You're standing
now, which is good, but what if I weren't?
If it happened to you lightening strike like
really really fast and was mostly painless
I guess that would be But still bad like still
like nevertheless in kinda like he be no
where way. Nevermore found. By
somebody, a custodian or whoever has to
find you there sitting or squatting or you
know just not standing and and your limp,
deadless life body on the toilet and
your limp dead dick just hanging there.

SELF PORTRAIT #2

Some poo probably still a little ensconced in your ass crack cuz you didn't have time he don't think to wipe or flush, before you... But, but maybe you did or it was natural or somebody was there with you holding your hand, so don't worry bout it. Or doo. Worry about it. (*Beat.*) Lots of people you know have actually they've um been struck down in the bathroom without somebody beside them to — and even there's a web website people, like Elvis. Whitney. Orville. Redenbacher.

Sips water.

SPEAKER   There's a website and you can see all of their faces the ones who have...
I knew them not not personally but at least the internet knows shows me their faces and names I know their them sort of people like kinda like how you know me sort of I exist somewhere surely beyond buzzfeed for sure. I think. Aand I just he ah we just never heard of it I bet because you know the F.B.I., and the men in black and the uh the um women in black and uh, but not you know not not Black men. I never heard of uh black men who died in a toilet. But did, maybe? Of natural causes there, perhaps, I don't — Has, though, who dies of natural causes? My grandfather. So. One. I guess some old people some old people they do die

of natural. Some old black natural men, they
doing nothing just, natural, living. Like
my grandfather my grandfather he died, so
naturally. Asleep, a few years ago of of of.
And that was a shock, unexpected though
he was more than just old. And Black. And
a man, he was more than that. (*Silence.*) I
am glad though. He didn't die on the toilet.

KICK BOOM   KICK BOOM SNAPPER
     KICK   BOOM   KICK   BOOM
SNAPPER KICK BOOM KICK   BOOM
          SNAPPER   HYPE MAN
   POP UP   POP UP

HYPE MAN gets hype, unseen.

KICK   BOOM KICK BOOM   KICK   BOOM

SPEAKER   So speaking of limp dicks him you know
I have a very small penis and that may come
as a surprise or not uh um to to some of you
because you've seen it and you know might
be inclined to disagree in general with the
police but I think probably on average he
probably has a very small penis and the size
of the penis is a difficult thing to to live with
sometimes but a large penis is also a
difficult thing to live with which is I believe
why is men generally speaking have it
so hard in here in this place, toilet bowl of
America, as someone once mentioned

SELF PORTRAIT #2

once and random and Black men of course
to have a small penis secretly is less
emasculating then sharing with a room full
of strangers this fact openly that, that
you have one which is but I I should say
that though she she allegedly has a very
small penis it must also be made known that
I have a veeeeeeeeerrrrrrryyyyyy tight
asshole. So (*Balancing gesture.*) it can be and
has been hard for me thus... to push. things.
out... and, especially difficult sometimes to
be there on the toilet, and the dating scene
sometimes some um because people judge
and people and youyou can more easily
show someone the size of your scrotum
than you can the the the incredible tightness
of your anus. And you know Ladies, am I
right? I mean I mean just imagine your-
selfves that you're out on a date and you
know your dick pops out of your pants
trespassing on the scene in uh uh moment of
call it passion say and someone's sort of
there looking at it someone you know your
date he meanwhile the entire time is you're
the one there thinking in your head if you're
aware of your "inadequacy" and maybe
even saying to them out loud No No No
Nononononononono it's uh Don't Be Alarmed
I have a tight anus and my penis popping
out for you to see was not meant to be rapey
or even meant, an accident but you know
but talkling about it will and with a little

sprinkle of hope, and honesty, and talking, and Beyonce that'll it'll will'll get us through I promise just JUST trust me people. And. All I'm saying is do and don't be so quick to judge.

Sips water, the toilet flushes.

      HORN   BELLS BELLS   BELLS BELLS
     HORN   BELLS   B E L L S
HORN   HORN
      BELLS BELLS BELLS
HORN   CLAP CLAP CLAP
CLAP CLAP CLAP   CLAP CLAP CLAP
     HYPE MAN   HYPE MAN GETS
                              HYPE
   HYPE MAN   HYPE MAN

HYPE MAN   HYPE   MAN

SPEAKER   Is there a condom for life-experience? Like a way to protect yourself from the world — because I'll wear it. I don't want to wear it, but I will. Actually I'm a fan of tight things I can be I'm a real big fan of a lot of things like that you know like crawl spaces and I really like a good you know for I like a treehouse I like him being up there you know like it's living I'm a teenager remember just living your life you know up in the clouds head held high when we were and I was once with wants and I was

ambitious and made it out of my hood
somehow even that, the tightest of spaces,
you know? All the things of the things
that I remember all it is the things of the
memory from my time when I was young
and all the things that you know was
were and was special to me and one of the
things was tightness and keeping your shit
tight being tight with people and and
and some of them are no longer with us.

Sips water, the toilet flushes.

SPEAKER   By tight, I mean: (*Gesturing, fingering a hole.*) Like that and and who doesn't like a bit uh that you know, pleasure? I know that — is this clear? I feel like it I like even in my doing my fingers like this you know in this in this ways because you might get the visual better or to take maybe you if you prefer two fingers I can (*Gesturing, two fingers touching as penises.*) just do this with it. Or even (*Gesturing, two fists touching as vaginas.*) And that that's it LIFE pleasure that that gives me pleasure that gives me a kind of joy that is unspeakable, gestural, guttural, and, you and I knownow how that feels or would have coulda now that he's dead who's gonna you know take care of his family and watch out for them? (*Silence.*) In tribes in South Africa did you know when you kill

someone's husband you have to take care
of his wife and family? (*Beat.*) Who's gonna
do that here is. To her when he's gone is
the officer going to comfort her and to to to
call his family and put his kids through
college and you know fuck his wife if that's
what she wants you know what I, I mean, I
was with this one girl once this one girl
at her place and we were about to, hopefully
(*Gesturing, fingering a hole.*) and and she was
like he he looked like a devil coming
towards me and I was like hold up I don't
even know you not yet I don't not how
you can never know anybody by one
Instagram you gotta get the bigger picture
— but maybe you don't do you? And that's
the funny thing about perception and its
and that's its my issue mostly my problem
probably I can't prove it to you, I'm not
an actor. And neither was he but maybe you
that's the world that you live in. The cloud,
clouds. Security! Just, click and shoot.
Upload my feelings to the cloud and then
you'll be happy all the time no one can
ever get to you that way, hide your insecurity. Keep your shit tight, mama used to
say. And I do, I try. I've learned ways to
ahm to to accommodate this life. If you want
to be here. (*Silence.*) Do you... wanna
be here? (*Beat.*) Live with it, It's how it is,
What else is there, Even condoms aren't
100%. Make yourself comfortable, mama.

It's tight in here but youre inside of it,
though. Though some folks prefer to pull
out.

Sips water.

SPEAKER (*Smiles.*) If I were a play and if that play
were performed by only me well
then that would be what we call: an
All-Black Play.

Sips water.

SPEAKER So about a day ago I was at was having
dinner he was at a friends house at a friend
of a friends house and chilling and playing
video games it it was you know was kind
of a nice thing I mean I wore a tie and the
house well because the house it was in
Connecticut and it was in the big house,
a big house like one of the big houses on
one of the wide streets and you know with
a fenced in yard and I felt safe because
I had the cilantro in my hand and I was
there walking not running, so. Well done
already. I did officer, I took my legs very
slowly from place to place to get to there to
where I was and when you got there he
was like wow this house is big and I mean
this is really an impressive house in many
ways you can see while walking through it
and. A kind of, it was kind of you you

know there was artwork on the walls, and
and furniture and. It's in Connecticut so.

Sips water.

SPEAKER   And we think, I failed to mention this
dinner where we were was intended was
being held for a very prominent figure
of us of of us writers it was HE was South
African the writer of plays of note And
white. A South African white. Well the
evening went on and on and everyone was
had been drinking wine that was warm and
and well as it happens when alcohol or mar-
ijuana is involved, or is found in his system
after the fact something something was
about to pop off and that something was in
addition to the cork from another bottle
of exquisite South African white the topic it
had been changed very suddenly to to
the racial politics in South Africa (*Silence.*)
Now this was in Connecticut. So clearly
everyone was going to have an opinion and
was going to share, to talk about it and
and the amount of alcohol we had consumed
meant that we were very very happy to
speak and perhapsing happy is not the right
word rather we felt obliged and tipsy
and desirous to. We Americans had a right
to speak. Or to remain silent, depending
on who you were. And you know in a play,
at least in a not-all-Black play with two

South African whites and other people
becoming delirious... Well...

Sips water.

SPEAKER   And the prominent South African white
who we were all there to drink and celebrate
was dry, and silent. And this disquieted
me somewhat. But, well, not too much
because you know it's a nice house and
there's art to distract me from my feelings if
I want, and at this point the hostess? or,
matriarch? the lady of the house who is was
an actor once they she then stood up
and said — well she didn't stand he sort of
stood-sat, like this, like perching over a
toilet you don't really want to sit upon — up
a little higher on up in the seat very confi-
dently as if in as I own this house and sort of
like sort of I made this food and I have
something to say and this is my theatrical
voice so we listened everyone did and
out came a story about a play, one in which
she had performed. And that play wasn't
really the point of her story but there was a
line in the play that she really wanted to
share with us which I will now share with
you — (*Clears throat.*) that line was: in
reference to — this is not the line by the
way this is a bit more preface — her
reference was to a black artist in a room
making art in a room surrounded by people

— People, the line from this that play was, this. The line: "everybody has their nigger." (*Silence*.) Now. Normally, I am not one to pause. And let me just say I, I did not put that in context just now, and not to act or act indignant but as a point of of clarification I not myself accustomed to being in this position. At dinner parties. In Connecticut. I don't know any prominent South Africans, I only know my own experience in Connecticut and who knew there is where you find people throw around the word faggot or kike at dinner parties whether it's in a play or it isn't. And I'm dead, I can't hide it. My face is my face. Naturally. I'm dead but I hope not. Some thoughtful, silent, exchange was to follow. But there was no reckoning. And and me meanwhile I thought I must be in a play this is not for real. Or in a dream — or a nightmare — and I should simply splash myself with with

Splashes their face with toilet water.

SPEAKER but, naw, that didn't work. I wasn't I don't find myself being. Though I am there. On the furniture I thought while sitting next to this prominent South African white on one side and the hostess matriarch actress, on the other side surrounded by, frankly, non-niggers. Did no one else have anything

to say? I wondered... wait. Am I the nigger
in this situation?

      PUSHDOWN   SYNTH
SYNTH   SYNTH   SYNTH   SYNTH   SYNTH

SYNTH   SYNTH   SYNTH
      GUNSHOT   GUNSHOT   GUNSHOT
SYNTH SYNTH SYNTH
SYNTH   SYNTH   SYNTH
SIREN   SIREN   SIREN

HYPE MAN   HYPE MAN GETS HYPE
      HYPE MAN   HYPE MAN

HYPE MAN   HYPE MAN

Sips water.

SPEAKER   Because of course we don't have forms of apartheid here in the United States.

Silence.
The toilet flushes.

SPEAKER   About a minute ago I was still here. Now I'm gone, I don't know where I am. I'm not an actor. This is not a play, but like a play everything is ephemeral. Even I am. By that I mean, I ah, what I want to say is... is... that we have some and well that's the what she was and I I I well sure but you know

you you and of a sort of whatyoumacallit
is and that well that what she she he said to
to, to before it all just and I orgy but never
with you know and of course we can be
a woman I can but but but butts and there is
one that was happening another way I
I couldn't put it past him or or it its and and
theres a a a uh you know you know you
know you know you you you you you you
you you you you you you you you you
you you you you you you you you you
you you you you you you you oh oh oh
you you you you you you you you you
you you you you you you you you you
Oh. Ohhhhhh, Now I remember

SYNTH SYNTH   SYNTH
     SYNTH   SYNTH   SYNTH
  SIREN   SIREN
    SIREN

END OF PLAY.

Self Portrait #5

a Ceremony;
a Sculpture;
a Play in four parts

MATERIALS

Part 1
Pliers and protective gloves
16-gauge metal coil
Bag of flour
Mixing bowl
Water
Table salt
Mixing spoon
Newspaper
Oven, or hairdryer, for heat
Personal effects; remnants from your life;
organic and non-organic, tangible and intangible
(ex. nail clippings, loose hairs, skin follicles,
thoughts of inadequacy, a frightening memory,
a small photo, etc.)

Part 2
Pencil or pen
Letter paper

Part 3
Scissors or knife
Paste (from part 1)
Quick drying black spray paint
Quick drying polyurathane
Black glitter adhesive or other subtle shimmers

Part 4
Mercy

PART 1: RITUAL

Turn on some music you love (perhaps sounds which are calming... whatever that means to you);

Collect the materials, including some organic, nonliquid personal effects (ex. nail clippings, loose hairs, skin follicles, thoughts of inadequacy, fear, etc.)

Wearing protective glove, use the pliers to cut the length of six feet of the sprung metal coil

Using the pliers, shape the cut coil into a hollow cavern, freeform sphere / globe / reverse-teardrop / funky ellipse, approximately 2-foot in length, 2-foot in diameter, with a tapered, playful, freeform width; your shape should have no representational features; allow it to be rough-hewn, infinite and wild; this frame is the armament for your eventual sculpture / soul

Mix the flour and water and salt into a light, glue-like paste (a papier-mâché)

Cut strips of the newspaper; dip the strips, one at a time, into the paste; wipe off excess paste and place the strips around your armament until it is fully covered by a layer; once finished, you want to dry the layer quickly, either by using a fan, hairdryer, or by placing it in the oven at 200-degrees for approx. 20 minutes, or by laying it out in the sunlight to strenghten and crystalize naturally

PART 2: OFFERING

Write a letter to your future self

Address the letter "Dear _____"

The letter should include:
a) a warm greeting
b) an expression of how your body is feeling right now
c) a private confession you've never shared with anyone
d) any specific hinderances you have too long-waited to let go of, or to disallow, or to move past
e) a pain or discomfort that relates to your personhood in America, and/or a short, personal anecdote that reveals this discomfort
f) the name of an individual, or individuals, who you want to forgive

PART 3: SACRIFICE

Take the letter and cut or rip it into long strips

Make a small incision in the sphere and place the strips of your letter and your personal effects (tangible and intangible) one-by-one, into the hollowness

Now, spray / paint the object using quick-dry black paint; dry completely

Once fully dry, spray / paint the object with polyurethane; dry completely

Add some small subtleties (black glitter? black diamonds?) to give it a hint of shimmer

PART 4: SURRENDER

Invoke the offerings you have placed in your soulful sculpture

Breathe

Uplift or mount this sphere to be displayed high above

Breathe

Allow it to carry these offerings on your behalf, henceforth

Breathe, and let go.

END OF PLAY.

SELF PORTRAIT #5

Self Portrait #7

Players:	an INTERPRETER, Black, any gender and, a small group of SPECTATORS and, a public space/place with foot traffic and PASSERSBY
Note:	SPECTATORS, initially, should receive instructions as a group of individuals (as opposed to individually).
	Throughout, the INTERPRETER remains neutral, noncombatant, unbiased.
	The INTERPRETER should interpret and direct, but never physically touch anyone.
	The timings as listed here are approximate. God is in the details, and in the eyes, and in the silences.
	Don't rush God.

[00:00]

The INTERPRETER appears.

From a distance, the INTERPRETER looks each SPECTATOR in the eyes.[1]

Maintaining eye contact as possible, the INTERPRETER guides the SPECTATORS to the public space, if they aren't already there.

[00:50]

The INTERPRETER and the SPECTATORS arrive.

A moment.

INTERPRETER   (*To spectators.*) Would you mind to stand in a line please?

The SPECTATORS obey (or not) staring outward towards the INTERPRETER.

INTERPRETER   (*Mantra.*) Would you mind?

---

[1]   Throughout this work, the INTERPRETER should make eye contact with individual SPECTATORS where possible; the eyes relate the truth, despite the spectacle.

[01:20]

INTERPRETER Would you mind placing 18-inches between you and the person next to you? (*Mantra.*)
Would you mind placing 18-inches between you and the person next to you?

[01:45]

The INTERPRETER slow-paces, inspecting these spacing arrangements.

INTERPRETER (*Mantra.*) Would you mind?

A moment.

INTERPRETER Would you mind to take (*However many are needed.*) steps back, please?

The SPECTATORS back away from the INTERPRETER towards a wall behind them.[2]

---

2   A glass wall, or other reflective surface, is preferred though not required.

INTERPRETER   (*Mantra.*) Would you mind?
(*Mantra, slow-pacing, eye contact.*)
Would you mind?

[02:30]

INTERPRETER   Would you mind please to lift your hands, raising them towards the heavens?

The INTERPRETER interprets with their own hands.
The SPECTATORS reinterpret as instructed.

[03:10]

A moment.

INTERPRETER   Please would you rotate one-hundred and eighty degrees?

The INTERPRETER interprets.

The SPECTATORS turn around (or not). [3]

[03:55]

The SPECTATORS stand a moment...
hands upraised,
faces staring at the wall.

---

3   Should any SPECTATORS choose not to turn around, the INTERPRETER may ask them once or twice more to rotate before moving on to the next instruction.

[04:35]

INTERPRETER   Would you mind separating your legs, adding the width of 24-inches between your feet?

The SPECTATORS modify their legs.
The INTERPRETER drops their own hannds here, paces to inspect, and gently modifies SPECTATORS as needed.

INTERPRETER   24-inches between your legs and feet.

A moment.

[05:52]

A moment.

INTERPRETER   Please, place your hands on the wall in front of you.

PASSERSBY pass by.
A moment.

INTERPRETER   (*Mantra.*) Please place your hands on the
              wall in front of you.

The SPECTATORS place their hands on the wall.

[07:18]

INTERPRETER   (*Repeating as necessary.*) 24-inches
              between your legs and feet.

*The INTERPRETER modifies a few SPECTATORS'
feet.*

[08:04]

INTERPRETER   Put your forehead on the wall.

[09:12]

The INTERPRETER slow-paces.
The INTERPRETER inspects.

PASSERSBY suspect.

[10:36]

The INTERPRETER slow-paces.
The INTERPRETER lingers a moment behind each SPECTATOR, one-by-one.

The INTERPRETER attempts to stare into each SPECTATOR's eyes through the back of each head.

The INTERPRETER steps back.
The INTERPRETER silently spectates.

[11:57]⁴

[12:12]

Will the SPECTATORS disobey and disengage?
Will they, too, spectate?

---

4   If PASSERSBY ever speak to the INTERPRETER, there is no reply/response.

[12:48]

The INTERPRETER approaches a (white) SPECTATOR from behind. In the SPECTATOR's ear the INTERPRETER whispers.

INTERPRETER   (*Sotto.*) You can go now.

The INTERPRETER steps back.
The SPECTATOR steps away.

A moment.

The INTERPRETER approaches a new (white) SPECTATOR. In the SPECTATOR's ear, a whisper.

INTERPRETER   (*Sotto, mantra.*) You can go now.

One at a time, the INTERPRETER deliberately releases the (white) SPECTATORS.

The people of color are the only SPECTATOR(s) left.
One-by-one the INTERPRETER whispers into their ears.

INTERPRETER (*Very sotto.*) You. You. You can. You are remarkable. You come from a people who are remarkable, who have lived remarkable lives. Your body is a song. You are a poem. Your face is a work of art. Your soul is steady steadfast, fast. You are loved — no — you are the personification of love; love in the form of a human is what you are. If anyone anywhere ever tells you otherwise, they lie. They lyin'. You? You're the truth. Remember this. Remember yourself. You've been beheld. Beauty. Stand bold. Be held. Behold. (*Pause.*) You can go now.

After the final SPECTATOR has been allowed to leave, the INTERPRETER assumes the position: upraised hands and head against the wall, feet 24-inches apart.

The SPECTATORS spectate and/or depart.

SELF PORTRAIT #7

[14:50]

Alone, the INTERPRETER is reminded of all the citizens who stood here before.

The INTERPRETER is allowed not to remain neutral henceforth.

PASSERSBY spectate.
PASSERSBY spectate.
PASSERSBY spectate.

END OF PLAY.

Self Portrait #28

Players: one SPECTATOR
          encased and isolated in quiet contemplation
          amid a soft, slender black space

Note: a small, ascendant light in the distant;
          a narrow guide to the chair & soft black
          walls tapered towards the light;
          the space faintly shimmering

SOUL IN ISOLATION YOUR SOUL IN ISOLATION YOUR SOUL IN ISOLATION YOUR SOUL IN ISOLATION YOUR SOUL IN ISOLATION YOUR SOUL IN ISOLATION YOUR SOUL

CREEEEAAAKKKK...

SOUL IN ISOLATION YOUR INFINANCE

YOUR SOUL IN ISOLATION YOUR SOUL IN

ISOLATION IS INFINITE YOU

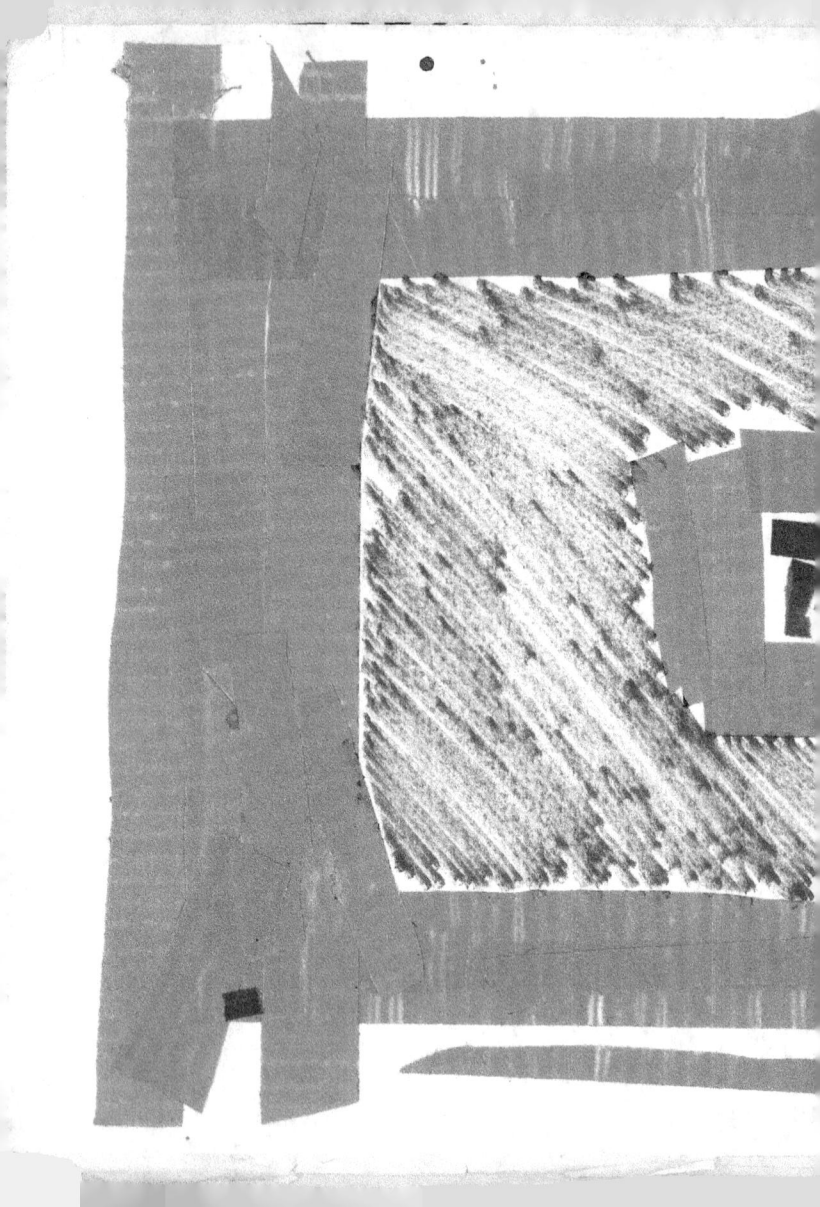

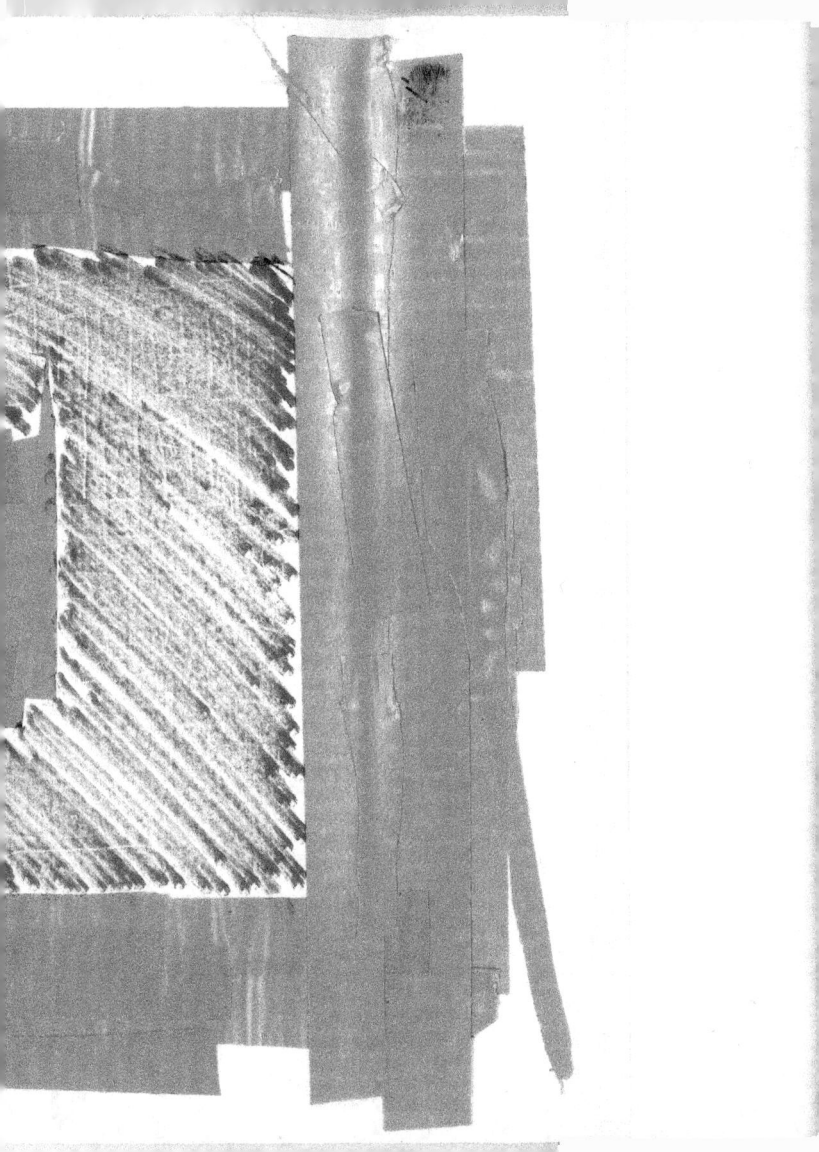

END OF PLAY.

SELF PORTRAIT #28

all of what you love
and none of what you hate

Players: GIRL A
           GIRL B
           MOTHER
           BOY

Neology: *Bbllbll,* a mouth-fart sound

           Hh, audible inhalation and/or exhalation (extended by the number of h's)

           N/ohn ohn, no

           Pst, small air pushed from the mouth

           Tck/tsch, tiny teeth suck

The spectators enter a dim, dark room. In a corner, unseen and unheard, a hooded figure sits. Bach fugues and preludes are playing.

MOVEMENT 1

A flash of light then nothing. From nothingness, the Bach fugues and preludes morph into a slowed-down, misunderstood version of The Anthem.[1] The Anthem becomes localized into headphones near the figure as —

---

1   The Anthem is an original, exquisitely over-produced hip-hop recording, the lyrics of which are only — and simply — the title of this play sampled and repeated, over and over in various tones and pitches.

MOVEMENT 2

The hooded figure takes off her hoodie to reveal GIRL A, listening to music. She switches on a single light. We see her, barely. Her clothing is a clash of color. She wears a lace-front wig under a hoodie. From her headphones, we hear the music. The music moves in and out of our hearing as she twice takes off her headphones to listen for the sound of something else.

Everything around the room is out-of-place, on its head. Standing on the wall, a desk is upturned onto its side.

Elsewhere, a single chair, like a picture frame, sets. A small stool hangs from the ceiling by one of its four legs. Also on the ceiling directly above the spectators, the bed hangs precariously upside-down, teddy bears and sheets pinned to it by magic. Scattered elsewhere: framed photographs, a floor lamp, a high school flag and a yearbook, hip-hop posters, a laptop computer. A small television set is in a corner.

GIRL A had been weeping. She had been looking at her phone. She had been pacing. Her sweat is visible, her breathing audible. Something urgent abounds. She turns off the light. She opens her cell phone and dials a number.

Silence.

The phone ringing. GIRL B answers.

GIRL B   (*Recorded.*) Hello? Hello??

GIRL A   Hey.

GIRL B   (*Recorded.*) Hey girl?!

MOVEMENT 3

Lights shift. GIRL B enters wearing a headscarf/hijab. Screen-grabs from the internet of GIRL B's popular social networking homepage are slide projected onto the wall behind her. She speaks directly to a spectator.

GIRL B Name: Ayesha.
Age: 15.
Favorite Books: Starburst by Portia, Super Flyyyy Girl by 'Miss' Latanya Little, Soul Sisters by Jeremiah Jackson, Jr., and The Quran.
Favorite Magazines: Black Hair!, and You Weekly.
Favorite Food: Sambuusa.
Heroes: my parents, and Michelle Obama.
Zodiac: Gemini. Deuces!!
Occupation-slash-Job: professional student.
Affiliations: J.R.W. High School. Red & black, what what yee-yah.
Future Ambitions: to become a better Muslim, to go to college and to make my parents proud, and, maybe (*Sotto.*) to become a model — Or, a famous dancer like the ones in music videos. (*A snippet of a notable hip-hop song plays as she dances.*)

Lights shift. GIRL B on the phone sings. She grabs at the hands of spectators as if on stage at a concert.

GIRL B (*To GIRL A on the phone.*) Come on girl sing it with me! (*Continues singing.*) You can't see but I'm doing my runway.
Come on, I know you know the words.

GIRL A is silent as GIRL B sings.

GIRL B (*She stops, giggles.*) What up Creeeep?

GIRL A Nuthin.

GIRL B —. Uhn-huh.

GIRL A What?

GIRL B My moms is always saying sumthin's usually up when people say 'nuthins up,' so.

GIRL A Yo mama.

GIRL B I know, right? You and me both. I love my dear mama like Tupac said — who doesn't? But sometimes, I'm like: Yo, mama (*"calm down"*). Am I right?

GIRL B practices her high-jump, at will, throughout.

GIRL A —. Righ—

GIRL B — I'm right. But you wrong, whats the deal whats up with you you win the lotto?
Quit school?

GIRL A   Naw.

GIRL B   Where you been?

GIRL A   —.

GIRL B   Hello — ? — You. Bean, at. Yesterday Today?

GIRL A   I wasn't. Feelin good is all, so I —

GIRL B   Phst, let you tell it. Trying to get outta writing that short story? I know I wish. After lunch — yesterday — I had had some real funky stuff happenin all up in my gut — prolly that cafeteria pizza — and I was at the bathroom for like my whoooole free period. Sorta fell sorry for whoever had came in there after me, boop. But that was yesterday what about you, and today, I couldnt find you out nowhere. Be-tee-dubs, my stomach is fine — thank you antacid! — but that short story is past due. Wait tho — did you get a extension? I bet. I know how you be, but you ain't usually late Miss A, scuse me Miss A-plus. Me I'm uh B and barely which is why I called AND I waited before realizing you wudn't late you just musta forgot. Remember? Was posta help me out before the track meet?? You know I cant see no needles, dang. Girl dang. I got fifth place. Outta five.

GIRL A   Like I said I wasn't feelin it —

GIRL B   Cap! Ohn ohn, I know you.
         You. Get. Cold feet

GIRL A   —. Yeah, whatever. Sorry

GIRL B   Sorry, see?! Cold feet, I knew. Well, you better
         slide on some socks and come on. These
         girls ain't playing they play sport for blood. I'm
         trying to win up in here, I need those extra-
         curriculars. To bump up my G.P.A.? By any
         means necessary that's what my daddy said:
         By. Any. MeanssSa. So. Even if that meanS a
         little poke in the leg. I'm trying to get this
         high JUMP. You too. Well, with swim-team-
         ing and whatnot. All that freestylin and
         breast-stroking, and breath-holding — I can't
         even float. You might as well be a fish, AND
         smart. Between that and school you gonna get
         a scholarship Miss A. Plus, might be a
         valedictory — heh, I said dick. As for me,
         I'm small and so are my grades, I need help.
         Nevermind with track & field? That's not a
         water-sport; that's blood-sport! These girls be
         jumping like frogs. Its just a little needle. After
         all they don't test us, not for no testosterone
         they don't. And anyways I'm not dumb, we do
         be passing tests don't we? That, we KNOW
         how to do. Right? We passing tests like, like
         a fatass be passing gas — Bbllbll, like that,
         Like. The salt across the dinner table, like 'this

ham needs some salt, can you please (*Pass.*)?'
Except that you know, in my house: halal. But
passing class? O it's gonna happen. Inshallah!
(*Jumps high.*)

GIRL A   (*as in Ayesha*) Esh —

GIRL B   Speaking uh happening, did you see the
cover of the new You Weekly, the one with
Magdalena on the front page looking like
(*Face.*) "Babies, Lies and Scandal!" Can you
believe she's been cheating on Lil'Money
like that, wha —? I would never — and on
Lil'Money? — nohn ohn. No. Me, I would
let him have my whooole heart —

A beeping sounds. It is GIRL B's call waiting.

GIRL B   O wait hold up, lemme get this...

*GIRL B clicks over to answer her other call. Silence.
GIRL B returns to the call.*

GIRL B   Whatever. Hello? —. Hello?

GIRL A   Hm?

GIRL B   Guess who that was? —. —. Him!

GIRL A   (?) who?

GIRL B   You know who.

GIRL A   O, but. I thought he was —

GIRL B   He is I am We was We were. But that nigga keep tryin to get at me. What I need is to pass these boys like salt, like gas. Like Lincoln freed the slaves, like — GO AWAY! — you're free, Now. Leave me alone.

GIRL A   But. You ain't got caller i.d.?

GIRL B   Yeah, but. He keep switchin numbers with the phone company tryin to fake me out and shit. Like some espionage.

GIRL A   Um. Listen Esh. I wanna —. I need to, tell you —

GIRL B   OMG, I just remembered what I remembered I wanted to tell you: You shoulda seen Shauna to-DAY. Awwe. What she had on — Sooooo What Not To Wear. She looked like a piece of hot-nast-eee. Ww. O what else I wanted to ask you — O yeah, you saw that text from Seline right? I was just, you heard what had happened to that girl Adriana? The one who sit in front uh me in Math?? The one wit the sideways ponytail one??? Yyooo, that chick got expelled, kicked alll the way outta school. Cuz I guess she was involved in some gang-type shit or whatever tryin to be all hard or whatever while meanwhile I did think she was a dyke but — Cap! — I was

wrong. See, Seline she said she heard the girl
was giving head down in the boys locker
room on her knees like communion. Yeah.
Like church in the wild, like. Woo child!
I can't. Can you imagine — ? — if it was us
they was talking bout like that. Just. Yeah.
No. Ohnohn. Boop, girl now lissin I gotta go
I gotta take JonJon to the liberry real quick
to return some of these books. You know,
them 'little learners?' My baby bro is startin to
read. It's kinda cute. And he gettin better
at it too, Inshallah. I love it. Girl you know me,
Imma good listener.

Silence.

GIRL B   You there?

GIRL A   Yeah —

GIRL B   Ok I gotta go. Call me tomorrow. A'ight?
Talk later. Mwah.

GIRL B exits. GIRL A hangs up the phone.
Silence.

MOTHER   (*Offstage.*) Hey, these dishes are still here in the
sink? You heard me in there?

MOVEMENT 4

Lights shift. MOTHER enters.
A screen-grab of photos from MOTHER's internet dating
webpage is projected onto the far wall.

MOTHER   Name: Deborah.
Age: 31.
Favorite Television Shows: I don't have
a chance to watch much TV, but. When I,
I enjoy all kinds but, especially reality.
The real. Especially, like, Real Housewives.
Religion? Christian.
Books I Am Reading: Dr. Johnny's Twelve
Steps to Growing Up, Growing Old and
Living Healthier: America's Most Renowned
Dietician Gives You Timeless Tips to
Live Longer, Look Better, and Be Great
at Any Age by Johnny Templeton the Third,
Ph.D. And, How To Be In Love, Be Happy,
And Stay There by Janice Wong.
(*Holds up copy of the book.*)
What's Trending With You — ? — : Work.
—.
In Search Of: Someone. Good-looking.
And, with a job. Somebody smart, who likes
spending time with a real woman.
A family man.
What You Are Not Looking For: Smokers
Cheaters Liars. Fakes. Freaks.
A Secret: Well then it wouldn't be a secret
would it? —. Ask me. No. —. Okay.

Its not uh. Okay. I like almost every daytime
TV talk show ever made. I record them to
watch later I have thousands of hours.
Secretly, I wish there was uh entire daytime
TV channel that showed only daytime TV,
even at nighttime. Just over and over again.
What else: I read a lot of columns. Like,
advice. In the newspaper, on the internet,
magazines, wherever. I even sent in some
questions of my own. And had two published.
That's right, I am a published author.
Twice. First question I ever had in print:
"Why do men and women want different
things from sex? Signed: Unsatisfied."
That was printed in a famous, local weekly.
I cut it out and put it in a frame on the wall.
—. Not over the bed. —.
More About Me: I'm a mother. I hope you can
handle that. I have two daughters. This is
my first time trying out something like this
and I'm ready. For whatever comes my way.

Lights shift. MOTHER exits.

GIRL A   I'll do them in a minute.

MOTHER   (*Offstage.*) You said you'd do them in a minute
forty-five minutes ago.

GIRL A   I'm in the bathroom.

GIRL A has old tears running down her cheeks. She walks into the bathroom and grabs a tissue to wipe her face and snotty nose. She returns and sits on the floor with her back against the wall. She reaches over and turns the television set on, volume low. She flips through the channels looking for something to watch. The channels vary: music videos, commercials, a daytime TV talk show fight, images of war, cartoons, pornography, an iconic clip from Real Housewives. GIRL A picks up the phone. She dials the number to call BOY. The phone ringing. BOY's voicemail answers.

BOY   (*Recorded.*) Yo, what up? This Quinell.

MOVEMENT 5

GIRL A turns off the television. Lights shift. BOY enters. With him he wheels in a turntable or other beat-making device. It remains here the entirety of the play. BOY begins crafting a beat as the animation of a live SMS text message between him and a girl is projected onto a far wall. The text reads:

yo whats up ?

                                                                  nuttin

s'what I wanna do

                                                                  ew u nasty

u like it

                                                                   :)

can I cum over

                                                                   no

!!!!

                                                                tomorrow

then u cum here

                                                             no, tomorrow.

BOY   Name: Quinell.
           Age: 17.
           Interested In: girls.
           Not Interested In: faggots.
           Education: G.E.D. research.
           Occupation: part-time grocery store bagger,
           part-time at-home-barber.
           Full-time: hustla. And too, aspiring emcee.
           Activities: cutting heads.
           Proclivities: making beats.
           Number of Shorties Currently Listed
           In My Cell: 83.
           Number of Haters: 0.

Lights shift to darkness. BOY exits.

BOY   (*Recorded.*) Yo son, leave uh message.
           I'll hollaback. One.
           (*Beep.*)

GIRL A   I need —. You need to — call me. —.
           When you get this.

*GIRL A hangs up. MOTHER walks into the room.
Light shines in from the hallway illuminating GIRL A who
sits on the floor.*

MOVEMENT 6

Silence. MOTHER turns on the bedroom's main light. MOTHER is barely older than GIRL A. MOTHER has a towel wrapped around her body and hair. She unwraps her hair which is wet from having just showered.

MOTHER Why you sitting in the dark? —. And what happened to the dishes? (*Pause.*) Hello?

GIRL A I heard.

MOTHER Yeah? Then why so slow to move. Your legs broke, hm? Fingers cracked? Must be cuz you said you'd do them. Thought when I got out the shower they'd be done. Yet the dishes remain. Downstairs. Dirty. Un-rinsed. Ruined. —. You ain't gone deaf and dumb have you?

GIRL A I just haven't yet.

MOTHER —. I know.

GIRL A I will I just. Haven't.

MOTHER What's the hold up? You were okay enough to eat. Looks like not much is happening up here. I do see is a lot uh <u>BLAH</u>. And, blah. Now I've said blahgain and again, blah is as blahh does. And we all have to do our part around here to blah BLAH. Putting off until

blahmorrow what can be done today is
irresponsiblah. And you know: Blah, blah-
blahblahblahblahbla. HezbullohBlah. B —.
Right? We spoke about that before?

GIRL A   I said I will. I will and —

Lights shift. MOTHER performs gestures[2] throughout the following speech.

MOTHER   (*To a spectator.*) She's not one to misbehave, but teenagers often do things like this. I read it in a column once. Twice. "Most teenagers, at some point in their lives, will openly defy the advice and authority of their parents and other figures of authority. The key to dealing with rebellious teenagers is avoiding confrontation, being patient and recognizing that you have a teenager. The important thing to remember is that most teenagers will pass through this phase and return to become normal law abiding citizens." I try my best to be the understanding one to understand. But a hardhead makes for a soft ass. I really don't want to have to beat her down. But that, too, is about love.

---

2   Variably: wags her finger; raises her hand to slap; folds her arms; shakes her head; her head and shoulders fall. Note on gestures: these are (mis)perceptions, stereotypes; each tick surprising the actor.

Lights shift.

MOTHER Baby. Whats uh matter?

GIRL A I just need —. A moment.

MOTHER Ok. What's the matter? You can tell me. You can tell me, I'm understanding. I was once like you Your age once not far from it now, Hm?

Silence.

GIRL A I'll do the dishes. I said I will.

MOTHER (*Pause.*) All right. All right. Well. Well. I'll leave you to it. Jerome — you remember Jerome? We're going out but we'll be back a little later on. Make sure to finish up your work. And homework.

GIRL A I will.

MOTHER And be sure to look after —

GIRL A I WILL.

MOTHER I'll call in uh while to check in on you. All right?

Silence. MOTHER exits through the door closing it behind her. GIRL A stands up and locks the door. She turns off the main light.

MOVEMENT 7

GIRL A turns on the TV. She walks into the bathroom. Though the images on the TV's screen are distorted, the following audio is heard from the television set. It might be the voice of an expert on a daytime TV talk show.

> Social and emotional abilities develop along with the brain, which continues to mature and take shape into the mid-20s. In adolescence, there's a period when a key part of this circuitry lags in its development. It's the prefrontal area, which plays a key role both in reading social signals and in inhibiting impulse to channel our emotions and social behavior in positive ways. This is why teens seem to be extremely impulsive and do things that they 'should know better' not to. So parents can help by helping teens think through social decisions and consider many alternatives and pick the best one, rather than just impulsively doing the first thing that occurs to them.

MOVEMENT 8

The phone ringing. GIRL A re-enters the room. She trips over the TV's electrical cord and it turns off. A light on GIRL B playing a hand-clapping game, solo, and chewing hard on a stick of bubblegum. GIRL A picks up her phone.

GIRL A　　Hello?

GIRL B　　Hey! What's up?

GIRL A　　Nuthin

GIRL B　　Awh now see. I knew it!

GIRL A　　Knew — what

GIRL B　　Anyway girl, you would nevah believe —
guess what? I just got back from the liberry.
I was with JonJon returning those readers,
and bout to checkout some new ones, right?
— when. I turn my back for one second and
he went an walkd off. I was dumb mad!
I'm lookin up and down the aisles, panickin
before I found him near that bank of
computers standin there next to some stranger.
Oooooo (*Through her teeth.*) I went right
over and snatched him up, apologizing to the
woman sittin there: 'Sorry, this is my
brother I hope he wasnt botherin you' —
And out the corner of my eye I caught quick
what she was lookin at. On the internet?

(*Pause.*) SEX MOVIES. Watchin sex movies — In the liberry! She was all click click clickin tryin to get rid uh the screen and I'm tryin to drag JonJon away. I walkd straight over to the counter to complain. And the man at the desk? He said there was nuthin he could do, that it was permissible. Something about privacy. Democracy? Public access to information — tck — I don't know. Then he said: 'Maybe she's doing research.' Ssgross. Last time I go to that branch.

Silence.

GIRL B   Hello?

GIRL A   Hey —

GIRL B   O I thought we got cut off I know what I wanted to s —

Long silence.

GIRL B   Bitch.

GIRL A   —. Hh?

GIRL B   Lying ass. Bitch.

GIRL A   —.

GIRL B   —. Francine.

GIRL A —. O.

GIRL B Fuckface Francine? That —. She is so mean.
(*Scoff.*) I can't stand that bitch. Lying Ass.
Telling lies spreading rumors. And, prolly
spreading her legs too — H! — wouldn't put it
past her. Guess what what Seline just texted me
Just now even I'm on the phone with
you? Francine trying me, AGAIN. Telling
rather, or what rather she said to Seline
was, dumbass prolly thinking wouldn't get
back around to me: 'she speaks so improper.'
Khh! — improper? And I happen to
knoooow, Francine? Got a Deeee last
semester, in English — no wait, D+

GIRL A Eesh —

GIRL B — in ENGLISH, which a D+ means
bitch you cant speak it so. And meanwhile.
I'm trying to better myself. Right?
And do my best to BLAH. By any blah
neccesaBLAH. Michelle Obama? Blah blah
— I ain't lyin! Blahbliss-ah-ah-ah. But Seline,
she be blah she blah. Blah! Blah blah blah blah.
Blahblahblahblahblahblahblahblahblahblah.
Can you believe that?

GIRL A I'm pregnant.

Silence.

GIRL B   What?

GIRL A   Pregnant.

GIRL B   How? —. I mean. O.

GIRL A   I took that pee test. The one from the pharmacy. The one with the lines on it. (*Pause.*) I failed. I peed on it and it was two lines, like a plus. Plus means pregnant.

GIRL B   —. (*Confident.*) Well. Well, maybe your pee was wrong.

GIRL A   Itsnot.

GIRL B   Well can't you go to a — I mean — or —

GIRL A   I don't know.

GIRL B   (*Pause.*) But —

GIRL A   I cant. —. I cant.

GIRL B   (*Pause.*) —. Who. By?

GIRL A   (*Silence.*)

GIRL B   Don't —. No we talked about —. Anybody but. But I thought you said all you two did was — ?

GIRL A (*Pause.*) What happened was —

Lights shift.

GIRL B performs gestures[3] throughout the following speech.

GIRL B (*To a female spectator.*) I told her not to be messing around with him. Him, him and his brothers they nothing but no good. And how do I know, my daddy told me that's how. Stay away from trouble he said. I said what and he said 'who.' Havent you heard the news? Hanging out on the sidewalk, niggas watchin the people and the cars come and go — what the hell is that all about? Can't be good can it? 'Isnt there somewhere else youre supposed to be son, in school perhaps?' They can teach you something cant they? Cant they? Make a new way insteada waiting for the world to pass you by, maybe. 'Suspect this isn't where you supposed to be, but maybe you wanna be though?' Living looking lost. Please. My daddy told me: 'Please not those niggas that don't wanna read. Don't wanna come to class. Please marry a nice policeman!' —. Ppht. This shit is so bum! —. —. Whatever. Artificial sympathy.

---

3 Variably: sucks her teeth; snaps her fingers; puts hands on her hips; stomps one foot; rolls her eyes. Note on gestures: these are (mis)perceptions, stereotypes; each tick surprising the actor.

Lights shift.

GIRL B   (*Artificial.*) Damn girl.
              What you gonna do now?

GIRL A   I don't know. (*Pause.*) hhhHhhnnnn.

MOVEMENT 9

GIRL B exits. Slide projection: Title reads,

what didn't happen:

followed by,

some weeks ago

Romantic 70's soul music plays. The desk has been turned into an elegant dining table. BOY appears at the door with a picnic basket. From inside the basket, he removes a bouquet of flowers, a bottle of sparkling cider, and two beef patties. BOY places all in front of GIRL A. BOY lights two candles.

BOY feeds GIRL A her food, as if they were lovers for a thousand years. GIRL A goes to the bathroom. After a moment, GIRL A reappears in the door to the bathroom wearing lingerie. She walks over and gives BOY a shoulder massage. BOY reciprocates by giving GIRL A a foot massage. They kiss. This display of affection continues throughout the next Movement.

MOVEMENT 10

Music dims. Lights shift. MOTHER enters carrying a newspaper. She reads from it the following quote aloud.

MOTHER Dear Holiday Blues, "Even if Mom was trying to send you a coded message — and I am not convinced that was her intent — you can turn the lemons of your mother's disapproval into the lemonade of a good, safe, responsible sex life. So Mom is not happy about her daughter being sexually active — that's too bad for Mom, right? Show Mom that her fears were misplaced by making sure you don't get your 19-year-old ass knocked up or knocked around. As for feeling like a pedophile, HB, there's nothing pedo about a 19-year-old bisexual chick in Disney-princess underpants. A little girl in those panties is innocent and darling. A sexually active 19-year-old in those panties is ironic and daring. (A quick poll of straight men — or man, as the sample size was small — also revealed that 100 percent consider 19-year-old bisexual girls in Disney panties 'sexy as fucking hell.') So when your boyfriend eats your pussy through a pair of your new Disney underpants — when he filters your vaginal secretions through an image of Jasmine or Ariel or Belle — he will not only be helping you assert your right to sexual fulfillment despite your mother's disapproval, HB, but helping you deconstruct a patriarchal heteronormative discourse that reifies female purity and holds up female undergarments as moral status markers. And when he services your clit, HB, the boyfriend will also be servicing those princesses. His efforts will transform them into the fully sexual beings their corporate creators never intended them to be. To think your boyfriend can accomplish all of that — and strike a blow against repressive monarchical systems, too — just by eating your pussy while you wear your new panties, HB! And all you have to do is lie back, pull the stick out of your ass, and enjoy." (*Pause.*) Well.

MOTHER exits. Music fades.

MOVEMENT 11

Lights shift. Slide projection: Title reads,

what did happen:

followed by,

some weeks ago

GIRL A is spread-eagle standing up against the wall. BOY's pants are around his knees and he bounces up and down on top of her. BOY looks inexperienced, a bit clumsy and juvenile. GIRL A bites her lip. BOY climaxes and lays atop GIRL A breathing heavy. BOY slinks to the ground. GIRL A pulls her panties up.

Silence.

GIRL A goes into the bathroom, pushing the door in slight. BOY pulls his pants up. He searches around for his things: ballcap, wallet, phone. The screen on his cell phone brightens as he checks his messages. BOY approaches the crack of light coming from the bathroom door. He speaks into the light.

BOY   Yo, I'm uh head on out, a'ight?

Silence.

BOY   Gimme uh call or sumthin, a'ight?

Silence.

BOY   Yo...... Yo...... a'ight.

BOY opens the bedroom door and exits.

MOVEMENT 12

Lights shift. GIRL B enters wearing a school uniform and carrying a backpack. From the backpack she removes leaflets promoting abstinence-only. GIRL B hands out leaflets to spectators. A recorded telephone bot that sounds vaguely female reads the following voiceover narration throughout.

> Welcome to: United States Department of Health and Human Services. Office of Population Affairs. Office of Adolescent Pregnancy Programs. Adolescent Family Life (AFL). Grant Programs for Prevention Demonstration Projects. Friends First: a newly-funded project originating in Littleton, Colorado
>
> The Friends First program provides two unique models of abstinence education programming. The STARS mentoring program is a cascading mentoring model using high school students as mentors/peer educators who deliver after school abstinence mentoring education to middle school — sixth to eigth grade — students.
>
> The Quinceanera program delivers culturally relevant abstinence education programming for twelve to fifteen year old adolescents and their families. The program evaluation will randomly assign participants and families in both programs into either the intervention

group or a control group that does not receive the intervention.

The evaluation will follow participants for up to two years post intervention.

Grant: $414,800
Contact: Gina Harris; 720-981-9193

Once GIRL B has given away all of her flyers, she exits.

MOVEMENT 13

ALL OF WHAT YOU LOVE ...

ALL OF WHAT YOU LOVE ...

MOVEMENT 14

GIRL A turns open the laptop. Light from the monitor fills the room. She surfs the web. The following typewritten texts appears simultaneously on a wall.

> Screen history, or Recently viewed pages: Adoption... Assistance... Alternatives...
>
> (*Type:*) www.google.com
> (*Press Enter.*)
>
> (*Type:*) abortion
> (*Press Enter.*)
>
> (*Scroll down.*)
>
> (*Type or click on:*) Abortion Facts —
> Information on Abortion you can use
>
> (*Linger on:*) Fact #1
>
> (*Scroll down.*)
>
> (*Scroll up.*)
>
> (*Click on:*) Get Help
>
> (*Scroll down.*)

MOVEMENT 15

BOY enters. He wears an apron and a nametag that bears his name "Quinell."

GIRL A picks up her phone. She dials BOY.
The phone rings. He answers.

BOY Hello?

GIRL A I've been calling

BOY Who this?

GIRL A Wh —

BOY O, hey, what up shorty.

GIRL A Don't WHAT UP SHORTY me. I been —

BOY Yo, I ain't got your number in my cell. Swhy I didn't pick up you know. You coulda been a bill collector. Yo I was busy — you know — takin care uh business.

GIRL A Whatever. Listen —

BOY Hold up. (*Pause. Sotto, to someone unseen.*) You want paper or plastic? Double it up?

GIRL A Hello?

BOY　　　　(*Sotto.*) One bag? A'ight then Ima just put this meat in here with this laundry detergent?

Silence. BOY returns to the phone.

BOY　　　　(*To GIRL A.*) Yo shorty what you was sayin now?

GIRL A　　We gotta problem.

BOY　　　　We? I ain't got no problem. Mo'money, mo'problems right? I ain't got no money so I ain't got no problems.

GIRL A　　I'm pregnant.

BOY　　　　(*Pause.*) You what?

GIRL A　　Pregnant.

Silence.

BOY　　　　So?

GIRL A　　(*Pause.*) So? —.

BOY coughs.

GIRL A　　So what??

BOY　　　　So What And? (*Sotto to stranger.*) —. Tips? Yeah thanks, appreciate it.

GIRL A   (*A questioning.*) And, nothing!

BOY   (*Back to GIRL A.*) Nothing's right. I don't know NO thing about that.

GIRL A   The shit you don't. Don't act retarded. (*A questioning.*) IT'S OURS DUMMY!

BOY   Yo, don't come calling me names and sh —. You better pump your brakes back to reality. This here, this is not about me.

GIRL A   —. —. I'll call you whatever I want and you — this isnt my fault. It's ours. We made this. We made this. We —

Lights shift. BOY performs gestures[4] *throughout the following speech.*

BOY   (*To a male spectator.*) Who she think she is accusing us uh some dumb dumb shit! Yo, we didn't even get down like that, son. I mean — we got down and I hit that but she telling stories. Me, Imma cautionary tale, I be creepin, yo. With them STDs and shit going round these days, I always make sure to

---

[4] Variably: grabs his crotch; adjusts his ballcap in an alternate direction; touches his facial hair. Note on gestures: these are (mis)perceptions, stereotypes; each tick surprising the actor.

wrap my big boy up. And because I get 'em free
from that fishbowl down at the supermarket!
(*Removes a roll of condoms from his wallet.*)
Look, I always roll wit sev-er-al, cuz, I meet
uh lot uh ladies and I ain't about to get caught
out there like that, son. Yo, I even make sure
that the expiry date is no less than 6 months
away cuz I can't be fooling around with no old
ass rubber now. Right?! Seriously, would you
put sour milk on your dick?? Word. Me
neither. YallknowwhatI'msayin. So ain't no god-
damn way that's mine, son. Hatin the player,
even though she played the game Ssshhhiiiit.
I'll tell you what though? Folks betta not go
around slandering my name or I'll set that ass
right. My rep cannot be fucked wit and I'll
preach the troof the whole troof and nothing
but. Yeah. Naw. (*Pause.*) Stop fantasizing
into me what I'm not.

Lights shift to darkness.

BOY (*Recorded.*) Yo, I'm at work I can't be talkin
I gotta go.

GIRL A	(*Recorded.*) What work, you ain't got no real job but you gonna have to —. Look better hear me out cuz I ain't about to —. The clock is... what the f—	BOY	(*Recorded.*) Yo, I don't wanna hang up on you all rudely and shit I gotta take care of business. And, you know the clock is ticking I'm on the clock, so —

The phone hangs up abrupt. Silence.

GIRL A dials BOY. The phone rings. BOY's voicemail recording answers. GIRL A hangs up without leaving a message.

GIRL A dials GIRL B. The phone rings. GIRL B's voicemail recording answers. Faint, in the recording's background, the hip-hop song from MOVEMENT 3, accompanied by the following:

GIRL B   (*Recorded.*) This is Ayesha's phone. Sorry I'm not around to answer your call. —. Wait — am I sorry? Psst. Let me think about it. Nope. I'm not. Because I could be busy and not around for any number of reasons, including that I might be tryin to better myself by studyin, or, I might be spending time with my real friends which is to say — the ones who ain't liars — or, I might just be ignoring you. So, if YOU'RE the one who's sorry and calling to say so, then please leave a message. However, don't bother if youre just looking for a shoulder, if youre uh victim of circumstance, if youre all excuses, if youre uh liar, uh stupid ho, uh poser, uh loser, uh idiot, uh —

A beeping sound. GIRL A hangs up abrupt. She tosses the phone onto the ground. Silence.

MOVEMENT 16

Whispers, strange and otherworldly. Preconception, sotto voce.

Primordial sounds. Gags, scoffs, groans, snickers. Perhaps, intermittent: snare reverb, kick-drum reverb, high hats. From the sounds emerge distinct VOICES.

VOICES	One two three four five six seven
	One two three four five six seven
	One two three four five six seven
	From nothing comes nothing.
	From nothing comes something.
	From nothing comes everything.
	The formation begins. The life within.
VOICE A	Yo mama so fat she eats Wheat Thicks.
VOICE B	Yo mama so fat when you get on top of her your ears pop.
VOICE A	Yo mama so fat she goes into a restaurant looks at the menu and says, I'd like to order all of that.
VOICE C	Yo mama so fat she has more Chins than that live in Chinatown.
VOICE B	Yo mama so fat even her clothes have stretch marks.

VOICE C   Yo mama so fat she cant reach her own pussy to finger it.

VOICE B   Yo mama so fat she fell in love and broke it.

VOICE A   Yo mama so fat her nickname is Fatass.

VOICE B / VOICE C   Fatass
Fatass
Fatass
Fatass

GIRL A grabs her headphones and puts them back on. She attempts to concentrate, bouncing her head to the unheard music as best she can.

A dark, hooded figure swoops in. Another hooded figure enters with a lit phone. They take a flash photo of the spectators.

The figures skulk, text, and scoff. They are grotesque.

VOICE C   Shit, this song.

VOICE B   This song is the shit.

VOICE A   This shit is bomb, underground like under the ground like sewage like dead people buried.

VOICE C   I know they talk a lot about fucking in this song, but really, this is about love. You realize that right?

VOICE B   Tsch. Naturally.

VOICE C   Not just love but like tribal. Like gritty and tribal and dark and danger. Like trap.

VOICE A   Oooh, that's that 'trap?'

VOICE B   Tsch. Naturally.

VOICE C   Nevahmind that the beat is fuckin ill too. Lissin to that shit. Smell that shit.

VOICE A   This is about love. You do realize that don't you?

VOICE B   O I know. That itty bitty nitty gritty-ness.

VOICE C   Bl-bl-bl-bl! It's about to pop off!

VOICE A   Thatdarkdangertribaltrapnittygrittyshittyshit.

VOICE C   Ya heard?

VOICE B   How could you not.

VOICE A / VOICE B / VOICE C   Word. (*Count-off.*) 1 2 3 4 5 6 7!

Lights shift. BOY removes his hood and pulls out a microphone from his back pocket. An unexquisite, homemade instrumental hip-hop track plays. BOY, overtop the track, raps freestyle.

BOY See I'm like, the baddest motherfucker in the
universe Got me ice on my wrist, went from last
to first When I chill like the breeze go
underneath they skirts I get to work, go to work,
make it work This ain't work, shiiiit ii ii i.

*GIRL B removes her hood and begins back-up dancing.
BOY ad-libs a bit, like: "I should get paid for this shit."*

BOY (*Still rapping.*) Listen, I like big butts and I
just cant lie I like'em young or old, them other
niggas just en-vie I'm so fresh so clean so
C-R-A-Z-Y So why hide my deeck with this
F-L-Y, be laz-I I I I I

MOTHER removes her hood and begins back-up dancing.

BOY (*Still rapping.*) I'm like blah blah blah blah blah
Blah blah blah blah blah blah blah blah blah blah
Blah blah blah blah blah blah blah blah blah blah
Blah blah blah blah blah blah blah blah blah blah

The last few "blahs" are sung R&B-style, in auto-tune.

*Lights shift. The VOICES return their hoodies to their heads
and slink themselves into corners of the bedroom.*

MOVEMENT 17

Silence. GIRL A turns open her laptop. She surfs the web. The following appears simultaneously projected on a wall behind her.

>(*Type:*) www.google.com
>(*Press Enter.*)
>
>(*Type:*) self-abortion
>(*Press Enter.*)
>
>(*Scroll down.*)
>
>(*Type:*) self-abortion + Tylenol
>(*Press Enter.*)
>
>(*Click on:*) "Self-Abortion: Woman took Tylenol, Motrin"
>
>(*Scroll down.*)
>(*Save in separate window.*)
>
>(*New window.*)
>
>(*Type:*) how to perform a self-abortion
>(*Press Enter.*)
>
>(*Scroll down.*)
>
>(*Click on YouTube video:*) "how to perform an abortion in 8 easy steps"

(*Scroll through with cursor.*)

(*Click to go back to Google.*)

(*Scroll down.*)

(*Click on:*) "self-induced abortion — Wikipedia, the free encyclopedia"

(*Click to go back to Google.*)

(*Scroll down.*)

(*Click back on:*) "Self-abortion: Woman took Tylenol, Motrin"

(*Scroll down.*)

(*Highlight with cursor:*) "... 30 Tylenol and five 800-miligrams Motrins ..."

GIRL A *puts the laptop down on the floor.*

She walks into the bathroom and opens the medicine cabinet. She searches for what she's looking for. The VOICES speak from their corners.

VOICE A   She don't get it.

VOICE B   She don't? Nope.

VOICE C   It ain't easy as 1, 2, and 3.

VOICE A / VOICE B   Ohn-ohn. Taint.

VOICE C   Can't float much longer. Better swim for shore.

VOICE A   Better find a buoy. Get up on it.

VOICE B   Get up on uh program.
Food stamps, E.B.T. card.

VOICE C   Accepted here!

VOICE B   WIC check. Free money.

VOICE A   Free food!

VOICE C   Accepted here! Can't beat free.

VOICE B   Free?! See. That's almost worth it.

VOICE A   Almost.

VOICE B   She's free. She's beat. She almost.

VOICE C   She's growed, about to be growin.
Stomach's slowly showin, so.

VOICE A / VOICE B / VOICE C   Mm. Mm. Mm.

Unable to find what she's looking for, GIRL A leaves her bedroom and walks down the hall to her mother's room.

Once there she rummages through the medicine cabinet and drawers for what she's looking for. We do not see her, but we hear her. She finds them: three large pill bottles of acetaminophen. She brings them back into her bathroom. She counts out the pills one by one. She pours herself a glass of water. She brings the water and the pills into the bedroom and sits on the floor. She looks at the pills. She looks at nothing. She looks at the water. She looks at nothing. She looks at nothing, she sees nothing. Nothing becomes nothing.

GIRL A   hhhhHHhhhh.

GIRL A turns to a photo affixed to the nearest wall. She touches it with her fingertips. She removes it from the wall. She touches the image of the figures in the photo. She hurls the framed photo towards the wall opposite. It shatters.

MOVEMENT 18

Silence. BABY SISTER in the other room whines. GIRL A rushes into the other room to check on her. Lights shift. Photo slideshow of BABY SISTER's pictures are projected onto a far wall. Between the baby's whining and goo-goo/ gah-gahing, a simultaneous translation is typed by a third party onto the screen. It reads:

> Name: Dondrea Alliyah.
> I am Baby Sister.
> I live in the other room.
> I pee and poop and whine.
> I laugh, and I do.
> I cannot read or write but I am a little learner.
> I smile, and I do.
> I watch and I doo.
> I cannot complete complex equations though maybe someday.
> I whine and laugh and poop and doo and do.
> I cannot understand you yet, but you think you know me well.
> I can make my eyes twinkle.
> I ignite wars.
> I can and I do.

The text fades. GIRL A brings the whining BABY SISTER into her bedroom. GIRL A rocks BABY SISTER.

GIRL A   Ssshhhh. Ssshhhhhss. Sssshh.
               Sssssssssssssssssssssshhhhhhh.

GIRL A hums BABY SISTER a song.

GIRL A   You wanna story? How bout uh story. Once upon a time, there was uh girl. Once upon a time she was a girl. Once upon a time she —. She —. —. She —

BABY SISTER quiets. GIRL A takes BABY SISTER back to her crib. GIRL A returns to her room and cracks the bedroom door so that it remains slightly open. She sits on the floor next to her pills. She lies down on the floor next to the pills. She stares at the pills. She closes her eyes.

MOVEMENT 19

GIRL B, MOTHER, and BOY sit amongst the spectators. They eat popcorn and snacks. BOY sips on a soda very loudly. GIRL B pops her bubble gum. Once again, they inhabit the VOICES.

VOICE A Tck tck tck tck.

VOICE B I knew. I knew it

VOICE C This shit here

VOICE A / VOICE B   Ssshh!

Silence.

VOICE C Ohnohn. (*Sotto.*) Don't go in the other room.

VOICE B I cant watch this. You playin yo type, Girl. Don't go in there

VOICE A Would you two please. Ssh!

VOICE B Bbbll!

VOICE C Nevah go in the other room, the deep end, not nevah alone

VOICE A It ain't that kinda story. This is a love story

VOICE C Swimming in the dark?
Something wrong always goes on

VOICE B Where you cant see. Whereshidden

VOICE C She should stay in here, I say. She should sleep on it.

VOICE A Kh! No she should not sleep. The shit just don't disappear

VOICE C Dumb-dummy not sleeping is what caused this shit in the first place.

VOICE B Popping that pussy. That's what caused this

VOICE A Ohnohn! T'was the guv'ment.

VOICE C Wha —? How bout all of it! Everybody and nobody.

VOICE B You don't know. Nobody knows

VOICE A (*Sings.*) "... the trouble I see." Bbbll

VOICE C This shit. What is this, a musical? Bet.

VOICE A A love story?

VOICE B Nonono nobody loves nobody.

VOICE C / VOICE A   Bodies just bodies

VOICE B   Shit happens

VOICE C   This happens just sleep on it. Everybody just go to sleep

VOICE B   Bbblll! Sleep on that shit in that bed you made it.

VOICE C   Just dream about it on it. Just fantasize your wade through. Just power pose.

VOICE A   She knows how.

VOICE B   How she, no, she should preempt the problem. Get nuclear. Drop a bomb. Like in those old-timey movies where everyday-type-folk take the law into their own hands? Shoot a motherfucker!

VOICE C   Itssnot western it's a horror, I think. Cuz me I'm skurred for her, chilllle. And for her child.

VOICE A   It's a tragedy! No. It's a Shame. No. It's a fable? Yeah. Yeah like, like Rumpelstilskin. But brown.

VOICE C   Could be uh comedy, tho. I cant say for sho.

VOICE A   I can! It's a neoliberal critique of the late stage American experiment in social decline. Clearly.

VOICE C   Dumb dumb this is drama. Dra-MA.
          Tis baby mama melodrama.

VOICE A   Dra-MAMAAAA!!

VOICE B   Well whateveh it is I still say she should shoot
          that motherfucker. Pop a cap in his ass.

VOICE A   Cap!

VOICE C   What she needs is a plan B.

VOICE A   Most people don't get mad about it.
          Most folks don't feel guilty or lash out, mostly.
          Not all but sum

VOICE B   Sum even get even, like:
          CapCapCapCapCapCap!

VOICE C   Stop doing the most. She ain't, is she? She's
          only almost.

VOICE A   Poor baby. She's not poor but, poor baby.

VOICE C   Why not sleepdream on it. There's always the
          morning after.

VOICE A   Out of body experience! That's what its called
          when you tryna get something outta your
          body. An out of body experience.

VOICE B   You fool. That's something else.

VOICE A   Well then. Look on the bright side

VOICE C   How so?

VOICE A   I dunno

VOICE C   Ooo I do!

VOICE B   Cap?

VOICE C   No... Gold. I know it's gross, but. Spin it. Spin your straw into gold.

VOICE A   You could be famous

VOICE B   Dumb-famous

VOICE C   Famous... PLUS! It's gross, but.

VOICE B   Negative but

VOICE A   A gross negative could be a net positive.

VOICE A / VOICE B / VOICE C   Mmmmmhmm

VOICE A   Sounds like that song:
"Brown skin girl stay home and mind baby
Brown skin girl stay home and mind baby
I'm goin away, in a sailing boat
And if I don't come back
Stay home and mind baby."
(*Pause.*)
What do you say?

Silence.

VOICE   (*Inflecting towards GIRL A, in varying tones and pitches.*)
Hey   Hey
   Hey   Hey
                                  Hey
      Hey   Hey-hey

HEY
—.

                Hey
   Hey.
  —.
—.
(*Flat.*) Dumbass.

MOVEMENT 20

Lights shift. GIRL A slinks to a corner of the bedroom. Slide projection #3: Title reads,

a hypothetical:
some months from now.

A home-video clip is displayed on the far wall. It is a silent film, excepting the movie music which underscores, dissonant against the scene. The scene, filmed by MOTHER, involves a very pregnant GIRL A wearing a do-rag and sweatpants. It is holiday time. BABY SISTER is playing around a Christmas tree. GIRL A is asking MOTHER not to film her in her current state. Nonetheless, MOTHER is filled with the Christmas spirit and continues filming away. She makes various comments about 'the meaning of Christmas' and 'the new addition' and 'becoming a grandmother too soon.'

The video ends.

MOVEMENT 21

Lights shift. GIRL A lays flat on her back, knees in the air. Music plays from the speakers of her discarded headphones. She grabs the pills and begins to swallow them slowly, two-by-two. Once finished, she goes into the bathroom. GIRL A leans onto the sink and washes out her mouth. She turns on the light above the sink in the bathroom. She opens up the medicine cabinet and takes out a toothbrush. She brushes her teeth. The VOICES, in their corners, spasm ecstatic. The walls begin to bleed red ink. The room shakes.

VOICE A   Faultlines.

VOICE B   Swallowed them bullets. Swallowed

VOICE C   Two-by-two. Swallowed your virtue

VOICE A   How about we astral project?

VOICE B   Down? Ain't nowhere left to but. To —. To —. To —.   VOICE A   Two-by-two-by-the-fistful.

VOICE C   How about we projectile vomit

VOICE A   Outta sight. Outta body

VOICE B   Outta mind

VOICE A / VOICE B / VOICE C   Faultlines.

VOICE C   Thought he was everything. And worth the love

VOICE A   Gave up. Gave in

VOICE B   Dropped a bomb in your belly and broke the seal

VOICE C   Surrendered, and now

VOICE A / VOICE B   The shame.

VOICE C   Who lost the war. You

VOICE A   Look who's left swallowing the bullets. That's who

VOICE B   Howd it taste? As good as his mouth done did?

VOICE A   Sgood as his lips?

VOICE C   What about his cock? You know you tasted it

VOICE B   She didnt! She choked!

VOICE C   O, she did. Tasted 'the D.' Plus.

VOICE A   Plus? His cum —? — You tasted that too?

VOICE B   Yep, she did do that. By mistake.

VOICE B / VOICE C   Mistakes were made

VOICE C	She swallowed	VOICE A	Ohn ohn Shut
	two by two		yo mouth —!
	by two		
	By two.	VOICE B	She didnt
	By two.		shut, she
	By two.		ShouldaCoulda,
	By two.		but didn't
	By two.		
	By two.	VOICE A	Bye bye right
	By.		down the well.
	By.		Ssyur own
	By.		fault. Right
	Bye. Bye.		down the

VOICE C Wellll whats done is done

VOICE A / VOICE B / VOICE C   MmhhMMm.

VOICE B Whats done is did, happens all the time

VOICE C Trying so hard to hold your breath

VOICE B Underwater for too long

VOICE A Damn him, son!

VOICE C Damn — her! She's damned

VOICE B (*To VOICE A*.) But what about YOU?

VOICE A What about me? This isn't about

VOICE B   He said she said

VOICE C   She said He said he had uh rubber, but

VOICE B   Cant put a rubber on the world, not over the whole world!

VOICE A   This isnt about —. This is about semiotics. This is about tectonics. This is about economics. This is about —

VOICE A / VOICE B / VOICE C   Naaaaawwww, son

VOICE B   War is a warrant unto itself

VOICE C   You're detained, indefinitely.
Indefinite detention, that's a bitch.

VOICE A   You tried to resist but temptation is a bitch.
A bitch, is temptation.

VOICE C   You wanted to get F'ed, right? Riiiight??

VOICE B   H! Shut yo mouth! Shut yo legs!

VOICE C   Not for nothing, you tried. You tried to resist but lost the war, dummy.

VOICE A   For trying, you get a D... plus an F.

All laugh.

VOICE B   In deed. Disobedience ain't civil, son.

VOICE C   Indeed. The deed is done.

VOICE B   Tainted!

VOICE C   Good girl gone bad. Gone sour

VOICE B   You know what youve done did is a crime in 47 states don't you?

VOICE C   Sex crime

VOICE B   Youre criminal. They'll get you for it.

VOICE A   Burn that witch!

VOICE B   Hang that bitch!

VOICE C   Acid burn that chick!

VOICE B   Done-done dumb-dumb. Delinquent.

VOICE A   Deprave

VOICE C   Shoulda slept on it. Shoulda prayed.

VOICE A   Still time to right some wrongs? Help yo'self. Make a call?

VOICE B   Backstroke? Belly flop?

VOICE A   Run from home runaway, don't walk. Runway walk.

VOICE B   Power pose! Lean in!

VOICE C   Sleep on it, put a ring on it! "If he like it then he shoulda" —

VOICE A   Naw shit on it. Bbbll! Sit on that shit.

VOICE B   Thatsit, sit on the toilet on it. Sit on the think tank.

VOICE C   (*Rapping.*) "Throw it up kid, I'm about to — throw it up kid, that's what I was born to do."

VOICE A   There's still time.

VOICE B   No. No more time. Not here. Time's did and done. Consequences come. And suffrage. The seal's been broken. Better find a shepherd, or else. Throw yourself right down the well.

Silence.

VOICES   (*Inflecting to the audience.*)   Weep not
Weep not   Weep not
                Weep   not
       Weep not
—.
You made this.

MOVEMENT 22

GIRL A screams. Silence. She emerges from the bathroom. Her hands are bloodied.

The TV turns itself on. Half of a child's face that belongs to SON appears. He speaks, but no sound is heard.

GIRL A goes to the television and smashes her foot in the frame. She punches at a pillow. She grabs a ball of crumpled up clothes, holds it to her mouth and screams into it. GIRL A unseen goes into the bathroom and pulls the shower curtain off of the bar. She throws the box of tissue around and rips everything out of the medicine cabinet.

GIRL A walks back into the room. She takes the chair from the wall and sits down on it. The lights swell. The phone rings. All is silent other than the phone. Ring. Ring. She answers.

MOTHER   (*Recorded.*) Hello? (*Pause.*) Hello??

Silence. GIRL A inhales quickly to speak, but is cut off by MOTHER's laughter on the phone to someone else.

MOTHER   (*Recorded.*) Hey honey, so we're going to a couple of other places, I wanted you to know. Hello? (*Pause.*) So, did you take care of what we talked about? (*Pause.*) I hope so. I mean, thank you.

GIRL A   Mama —

MOTHER (*Recorded.*) Baby, I'm sorry, I um — this is — I need to get this call on the other line — I — we — we'll be home in a few, K? (*Silence.*) Okay? (*Silence.*) (*Laughs.*) Okay.

The phone hangs up. A dial-tone.

MOVEMENT 23

A golden ring shines on GIRL A. Like a nimbus, she radiates.

GIRL A   My name ain't Girl. It ain't Shorty, or Ma. My name is Shantelle Monique. Johnson. 15 years old. I don't know. What it was I wanted. Or, I knew but not really. Or. I wanted, what they said I couldnt have. Joy. Freedom. Truth. Myself. —. —. Once. Once upon a time there was a girl. She lived. In a sand castle. Underwater. Surrounded by a beautiful, drowned kingdom. She wasnt a queen, she wasnt even a princess even. Just uh. Citizen of the sea. One day, she looked up. Saw the brightest of bright lights. Still there, right atop the ocean. Now she had noticed the light before, many many times. Often at night, she would sleep-dream a story. That light dancing arm in arm with the sea. A waltz. To a fugue. People in the kingdom knew well not to swim towards the light. For whatever reason its just not what was done. But this girl was a curious creature. One night, she snuck out from her blanket of sand. Kissed her sleeping mother goodbye and swam away, slowly, surely. Softly she swam towards the light. She swam curious of what to find on the other side of the radiance. She swam. Dreaming while awake. Imagining herself in a waltz with the sea. She swam towards the light. Slowly. Beginning to realize the light was no closer.

No closer but she, swimming further and
further away from home. Yet the light, still
there, warm. Still shining? A beautiful,
brilliant blaze. To be in that light. To feel its
beauty and warmth. She swam. She swam.
She swam. She —

Lights shift. GIRL A shifts, fortissimo.

GIRL A Yo son. Yo son, I seent you. I seent you on the
Looking at me, jocking me checking out my
Don't play. I seent you. Creeping up cept you
ain't know I did I did so what you want to do?
O, word? How old you is? Yo mama, yo
body is bangin. Drinkin that whole milk I see.
Stop playin I seent you lookin out yo side
eye, son. Say: it don't have to be about nothing
but what its about so. Lets be bout it then.

BOY enters and performs gestures in rolling repetition.
Lights shift. GIRL A shifts.

GIRL A My future ambitions? My future ambitions??
I pray so ambitions are irrelevant. I am not
who you think I am, No. I am NOT all yours
or what you imagine of me, but. Would that
ever be enough? Right. Riiiiiigght. Teachers,
Parents, Preachers all wanna holla my way.
Want me to whisper like, and smile sweetly
like, and be careful like, and remember to
hang back behind him while pulling the weight
uh the world. Right. Praying to you and

Allah on my knees? Nigga, please. Love?!
You don't even know the word. Go ahead
try Diggin it up outta all the other mud, and
mire and and, and keep trying to. Just wade
through. Wade through the terror through the
water through the shit through the —

GIRL B enters and performs gestures. Lights shift.
GIRL A shifts.

GIRL A   A hardhead makes for a soft ass. A hard head
makes for a soft ass. Don't get beatdown.
Don't be hard-headed, don't be a Stupidass.
Stupid-soft-ass-don't-wanna-be-lissnin.

MOTHER enters. Lights shift.
The Anthem plays. It's bangin. It's brutal.

Desperate, GIRL A bounces her head.
Music shifts. GIRL A jumps high. Lights shift.

GIRL A performs the Salah.
MOTHER, BOY and GIRL B jump high.

GIRL A   What I want? I wanna sing make you dance.
We gotta dance to keep from dyin. We gotta
dance to keep from cryin.

The Anthem plays. The room opens to reveal a spectacle of
light and sound. It engulfs and overwhelms.

MOTHER, BOY, and GIRL B are an exploded spectacle of gestures, handclapping, and high jumps. Everything is shifting except GIRL A who is shiftless amongst the spectacle.

The spectacle ends.
GIRL A steps forward into nothingness.

GIRL A   Too much. All of it. Babel. Tremors that used to couldnt shake the kingdom. Now is everywhere. And everybody. We afloat. All up in it. Not sure what to and what not. What I do know is: no more dreams deferred. Not to noise. Not to you.

The golden light grows.
GIRL A steps behind the beat-making machine.

She now takes control, improvising a brand-new rhythm that's all her own. The golden light grows, and grows.

MOTHER, GIRL B, and BOY continue performing their gestures as exiting.

The beat which GIRL A has been crafting continues now, on a loop, as she steps away from the beat machine.

GIRL A   This here this is about love. In spite of all of what we face. The future's still here. Right? You hear me. You see me? You feel me.

GIRL A embraces herself entirely.

Her entirety is love.

She begins to play a hand-clapping game, solo, as everything around her fades slowly to black.

GIRL A   Can't stop won't stop
Can't stop won't stop
Can't stop won't stop
Can't stop won't stop
Can't stop won't stop
Can't stop won't stop
Can't stop won't stop
Can't stop won't stop
Can't stop won't stop
Can't stop won't stop
Can't stop won't stop
Can't stop won't stop
Can't stop won't stop
Can't stop won't stop

END OF PLAY.

PRODUCTION CREDITS

Inquiry was originally published by Duke University Press in Volume 48, Issue 3 of *THEATER*, edited by David Bruin and Tom Sellar.

Conjecture was originally published by 53rd State Press in *OCCASIONAL No. 2*, edited by Will Arbery.

462 Halsey premiered as a part of The Motor Company's *Communal Spaces: A Garden Play Festival* in Brooklyn, NY, on August 27, 2016. The play was written for and performed at 462 Halsey Community Garden. It was produced and directed by Lillian Meredith. The cast was:

A   Aaron Morton
B   Timothy Craig

Self Portrait #7 was originally presented at the 15th annual PRELUDE Festival at the Martin E. Segal Theatre Center (Frank Hentschker, Executive Director), the Graduate Center, CUNY, in New York, NY, on October 9, 2015. The curators were Antje Oegel & Tom Sellar, and the producer was Eryk Aughenbaugh. The role of INTERPRETER was performed by the author.

Self Portrait #7 was later workshopped at Lincoln Center Education (Russell Granet, Executive Director) in New York, NY, on March 29, 2016. The role of INTERPRETER was performed by Jonathan Gonzalez and Oge Agulué. It was directed by Margot Bordelon.

Self Portrait #2, *Self Portrait #5*, *Self Portrait #7*, and *Self Portrait #28* premiered as part of *Self Portraits* at BRIC-Arts Media (Kristina Newman-Stewart, President) in Brooklyn, NY, on April 24, 2019. It was directed by Stevie Walker-Webb. The scenic and lighting design were by David Goldstein; the sound design was by Brian Hickey; the costumes were by Natalie Loveland; and the production stage manager was Leigh Walter. The producers were Zachary Elkind, B.J. Evans, Emily Harney, and Kelly Kerwin. For these works, the cast was:

SPEAKER	Michael Oloyede
HYPE MAN	Kyle Price
SPEAKER	Erin Margaret Pettigrew
HYPE MAN	Jillian Macklin
INTERPRETER	Blake Morris

all of what you love and none of what you hate was first presented at Yale Cabaret in New Haven, CT, on January 17, 2013. It was directed by Kate Tarker. The scenic design was by Portia Elmer and Mariana Sanchez-Hernandez; the costume design was by Grier Coleman; the lighting design was by Oliver Wason; the sound design was by Sang Ahm and Pornchanok Kanchanabanca; the projection design was by Paul Lieber; the choreography was by Jabari Brisport; the dramaturgy was by Helen C. Jaksch; and the production stage manager was Rob Chikar. The producers were Stephanie Rolland and Sarah Williams. The cast was:

GIRL A	Zenzi Williams
GIRL B	Tiffany Mack
MOTHER	Prema Cruz
BOY	Cornelius Davidson

all of what you love and none of what you hate was developed as part of the *RISK IS THIS… New Experimental Plays Festival* at Cutting Ball Theater (Rob Melrose & Paige Rogers, Artistic Directors; Ariel Craft, Associate Artistic Director) in San Francisco, CA, on March 11, 2015. It was directed by Margo Hall. The sound design was by Brian Hickey. The cast was:

GIRL A   Britney Frazier
GIRL B   Tristan Cunningham
MOTHER   Kimberly Daniels
BOY   Anthony J. Williams

all of what you love and none of what you hate received its world premiere at San Francisco Playhouse (Bill English, Artistic Director; Jordan Puckett, Associate Artistic Director) in San Francisco, CA, on April 31, 2016. It was directed by Edris Cooper-Anifowoshe. The scenic design was by Zoe Rosenfeld; the costume design was by Ellen Howes; the lighting design was by Sophia Craven; the sound design was by James Ard; additional sound and music composition was by Brian Hickey; the video design was by Brian Herczog and Laura Lopez; the movement direction was by Stephen Buescher; the props design was by Maeve Morgan. The cast was:

GIRL A   Britney Frazier
GIRL B   Tristan Cunningham
MOTHER   Indiia Wilmott
BOY   Cameron Matthews

PRODUCTION PHOTOS

all of what you love and none of what you hate at SF Playhouse.
Britney Frazier as GIRL A. Photo by Kevin Lin.

all of what you love and none of what you hate at SF Playhouse.
Cameron Matthews as BOY. Photo by Kevin Lin.

Self Portrait #2 at BRIC-Arts Media. Michael Oloyede as SPEAKER. Kyle Price as HYPE MAN (unseen). Photo by Edward T. Morris.

Self Portrait #3 at BRIC-Arts Media. Jelani Alladin as SUSPENDED MAN. Photo by Edward T. Morris.

Self Portrait #10 at BRIC-Arts Media. Leland Folwer and Ramad Carter as TWO LOVERS. Photo by Edward T. Morris.

Self Portrait #17 at BRIC-Arts Media. Jillian Macklin as PARENT and Kyle Price as CHILD. Photo by Edward T. Morris.

Self Portrait #5. Photo courtesy of artist.

Self Portrait #5 at BRIC-Arts Media. Photo by Edward T. Morris.

Self Portrait #7 at BRIC-Arts Media. Blake Morris as INTERPRETER and SPECTATORS. Photos by Edward T. Morris.

PHILLIP HOWZE is an American writer and theater maker whose works include *Self Portraits* (BRIC-Arts Media) and *Frontieres Sans Frontieres* (Bushwick Starr). His plays have been developed or produced at Bay Area Playwrights Festival, Clubbed Thumb, Cutting Ball, New York Theater Workshop, PRELUDE, Public Theater/NYSF, San Francisco Playhouse, Signature Theatre, Theater Masters, and Yale Cabaret. A graduate of Yale School of Drama, he is a Fellow of the Sundance Theater Lab, a Lucas Artist Fellow at Montalvo Arts, a 2021 Jerome Hill Artist Fellow, a MAP Fund grantee, a Resident Writer at Lincoln Center, and is under commission with the American Repertory Theater, the Manhattan Theatre Club/Sloan, and Lincoln Center Theater/LCT3. He was recently appointed the inaugural Associate Senior Lecturer in Playwriting at Harvard University's new Theater, Dance & Media program.

Photo by Beowulf Sheehan.

ACKNOWLEDGEMENTS

Thank you to Sheila Callaghan and Jacqueline Goldfinger for their advocacy to prompt this publication. Thank you to Sarah Ruhl for inviting and encouraging me, always. Thank you to Adithya Pratama who helped prepare the text. Thank you to the many brilliant actors, directors, designers, dramaturgs and artistic folx who gently shepherded these works from the twilight of imagination, through the valley, across the brook, and into daybreak.

And to my family, I love you. And to my teachers, I love you. And to my lover, I love you.

Rarities & Wonders: Plays
by Phillip Howze

Published by
Tripwire Harlot Press

Design by
Nilas Andersen
and Matt Wolff

Editorial support
from Gabby Preston

ISBN 978-1-7341402-4-8

Rarities & Wonders: Plays
is a part of the Sledgehammer
Series published by Tripwire
Harlot Press.

www.tripwireharlot.com

This book is made possible in
part by generous support
from the Jerome Foundation
and the MAP Fund.

An Ending

This is the very last thing I wrote for this book before it went to print. I write these words in real-time mere weeks before the final draft is due. No one asked. I write this not intending nor knowing it will arrive until there — boom! — it is. Some sudden new sense. Finality? Futility? An ending without needing or meaning to be.

Conclusions can occur in this way. By ambush, or dismay, or wander. Wherever one wonders. How and however it happens, I try to take notice. Writing is writing but creativity is rare. Emergent, or rather:

Like un-mining a landmine and looking at it.

You must dig. There's no other way to end but to begin. The inkwell is profound and the page is impatient. Your pen won't write itself into words, will it. Start to finish. Dredge. For something to matter it must have matter. For the end of a thing to matter its matter must end. Nothing in life is ordained except death.

Thus, endings take on eminence and awe.

Notice how certain endings throughout human history have come to acquire special designation. For example the end of a sentence — such as the one you're reading right now — is called a period. A final prayer or blessing is deemed a benediction. The term for end of life care is hospice. The necessary rites and celebration of someone's afterlife are known as a funeral.

This is understood. Which is why when an Asian grandmother, or a transwoman of color, or a political refugee, or a Black person is murdered in a residential neighborhood and their dead body left to rot in the street for the wondering eyes of children, any and all who wander there to bear witness will eminently understand — yes, even the murderer himself — that this is not how a life ought to end.

Though why then did it happen? And why does it keep happening with such convenience and consistency?

Take notice. Take care.

Careful submitting to the conveniences of those whose standards subvert your sense of personhood. Don't doom yourself to the expectations of outdated maps. To wander and roam is a human right. Forgo forgone conclusions. Happiness too, at times, can seem a canned ending deployed in service of ease, dilution, and delusion. Be more abiding. Pedetermined greater-goods too often end up tasting like dry goods. (Dehydrated hope isn't always healthiest.)

Dig deeper. Dip back into the well. Bathe in dreaming. Stay moisturized.

Beginning is easier because each of us has already done it once, with our first breath. Knowing when and how to end is hard. Which is why we have to feel it. Like tasting, touching, hearing and smelling — an ending is felt.

Feel about and you'll find it. Frolic. Have fun. Swerve in
exquisite wonder. Utter what Audre Lorde calls a sense of
satisfaction and completion.[†] At last, cry out a fullness.

And if all else fails you can always end things spectacularly.
Send them away with a bop and a dance. Or better yet —
bang! — let fireworks aloose onstage like it's the Fourth
of July. Write yourself all the way through to the end,
in freehand, with joy, conviction, gratitude, self-respect,
a stockpile of grace and wells of compassion:

[†]   Lorde, Audre. "The Uses of the Erotic: The Erotic as Power."
Sister Outsider.

These
Words are
a blessing

Like
John O Donahue's
but different

Quite
Quite grounded
Quite celestial

Same as
I am a blessing
too

It is
To have words
with you

Who are
A blessing
to

Carry
Us a cross
through

Angst
Toword forgiveness
hence

For this
I give
I give

Thanks
Thank you
for you

Bless me
Bless you
and

tripwireharlot.com

www.ingramcontent.com/pod-product-compliance
Lightning Source LLC
Chambersburg PA
CBHW071240070526
44583CB00017B/2265